SMITH'S

INTEREST TABLES

AT

FIVE, SIX, SEVEN, EIGHT, TEN AND TWELVE PER CENT. PER ANNUM,

SHOWING THE INTEREST

ON ANY SUM FROM $1.00 TO $10,000,

FROM ONE DAY TO FIVE YEARS.

TO WHICH ARE ADDED SEVERAL

VERY USEFUL BUSINESS TABLES.

CALCULATED BY

DUANE DOTY, ESQ.

PUBLISHED BY
E. B. SMITH & CO.,
116 AND 118 WOODWARD AVENUE,
DETROIT, MICH.

INTRODUCTION.

The percentage Tables in this volume have been prepared in the belief that they will be found very useful to business men everywhere.

TABLE I.—This Table shows the Interest upon One Dollar for one hundred days at the several rates per cent.; the interest being calculated to *five* places of decimals. By means of this table, interest may be computed very easily, the rule being to take from the Table the interest upon the One Dollar for the given time and multiply it by the number of dollars upon which you wish to know the interest.

Example.—What is the interest upon $200 for 91 days at 8 per cent? Take from the table the interest upon One Dollar for the time, which is............ .02022
Multiply the interest by................ 200

$4.04400

TABLE II.—This is the general Interest Table from which interest upon any sum is directly taken. At the top of each page is the number of Dollars upon which the interest is computed, as shown upon the page. The Time Column, showing the years, months and days, in their natural order, is in the center of each page, and the most common rates of interest, 7 and 10 per cent., arranged on either side of it, with interest at other rates arranged in parellel vertical columns.

Example.—What is the interest upon $500, for one year, four months and seventeen days, at 8 per cent.?

Turn to page 111, which gives the interest for one year, as $40.00
And for four months, as............... 13.33
And for seventeen days, as............ 1.89

$55.22

To get the interest for the cents, take from the table as for dollars, simply pointing off two more places of decimals in the result, the interest for a given number of cents being just one hundreth part of the interest for a like number of dollars.

TABLE III.—The use of the Compound Interest Table, on page 8 is as follows: The first left hand column shows the years from 1 to 20, and the horizontal lines to the right show the *amount* of $1, or £1, at compound interest, at the rates shown in the top line. These amounts are carried to six places of decimals. The rule is to take from the Table the amount of one dollar for the time and rate, and multiply it by the number of dollars.

Example.—What is the amount of $500, at compound interest, for thirteen years, at 4½ per cent.?

The amount of one dollar for the time as shown in the table, is $1.772196

Multiply by the number of dollars,.. 500

Which gives as the amount required, $886.098000

TABLE IV is a Table of per cents. to be used in the marking goods. On the left hand vertical column are given the numbers from 1 to 100, which may be regarded as the *cost* numbers; the other vertical columns show at what each article should be marked for selling, in order to gain the per cent. shown at the head of the columns.

Example.—At what must an article, which costs 44 cents, be sold, in order to gain 12½ per cent.?

Turn to 44 in the left hand column, at the right of it, under column headed 12½, we find 49.50, which shows that the article must be marked 49½ cents to secure the required profit. In marking goods, any fractional part of a cent upon the cost is considered a cent; for example, an article that cost 18½ cents, would for purposes of marking, be taken as 19.

TABLE V, page 130, is for finding the number of days from one date to another.

Example.—1st. How many days between August 1st and October 17?

Under October 17, on page 130, is the number 290; diminish this by 213, the number under August 1, which gives 77 as the number required.

Example.—2d. How many days from July 22d to the 12th of March following?

Under March 12, in second year, is the number 436. Subtract from this the number under July 22d, in the first year, which is 203, which gives us 233 as the number of days required.

1 Dollar.

12 PER CENT.	6 PER CENT.	7 PER CENT.	YEARS.	10 PER CENT.	5 PER CENT.	8 PER CENT.
.12	.06	.07	1	.10	.05	.08
.24	.12	.14	2	.20	.10	.16
.36	.18	.21	3	.30	.15	.24
.48	.24	.28	4	.40	.20	.32
.60	.30	.35	5	.50	.25	.40
			MONTHS.			
.01	.005	.00583	1	.00833	.00416	.00666
.02	.01	.01166	2	.01666	.00833	.01333
.03	.015	.01750	3	.02500	.01250	.02000
.04	.02	.02333	4	.03333	.01666	.02666
.05	.025	.02916	5	.04166	.02083	.03333
.06	.03	.03500	**6**	.05000	.02500	.04000
.07	.035	.04083	7	.05833	.02916	.04666
.08	.04	.04666	8	.06666	.03333	.05333
.09	.045	.05250	9	.07500	.03750	.06000
.10	.05	.05833	10	.08333	.04166	.06666
.11	.055	.06416	11	.09166	.04583	.07333
			DAYS.			
.00033	.00016	.00019	1	.00027	.00013	.00022
.00066	.00033	.00038	2	.00055	.00027	.00044
.00100	.00050	.00058	3	.00083	.00041	.00066
.00133	.00066	.00077	4	.00111	.00055	.00088
.00166	.00083	.00097	**5**	.00138	.00069	.00111
.00200	.00100	.00116	6	.00166	.00083	.00133
.00233	.00116	.00136	7	.00194	.00097	.00155
.00266	.00133	.00155	8	.00222	.00111	.00177
.00300	.00150	.00175	9	.00250	.00125	.00200
.00333	.00166	.00194	**10**	.00277	.00138	.00222
.00366	.00183	.00213	11	.00305	.00152	.00244
.00400	.00200	.00233	12	.00333	.00166	.00266
.00433	.00216	.00252	13	.00361	.00180	.00288
.00466	.00233	.00272	14	.00388	.00194	.00311
.00500	.00250	.00291	**15**	.00416	.00208	.00333
.00533	.00266	.00311	16	.00444	.00222	.00355
.00566	.00283	.00330	17	.00472	.00236	.00377
.00600	.00300	.00350	18	.00500	.00250	.00400
.00633	.00316	.00369	19	.00527	.00263	.00422
.00666	.00333	.00388	**20**	.00555	.00277	.00444
.00700	.00350	.00408	21	.00583	.00291	.00466
.00733	.00366	.00427	22	.00611	.00305	.00488
.00766	.00383	.00447	23	.00638	.00319	.00511
.00800	.00400	.00466	24	.00666	.00333	.00533
.00833	.00416	.00486	**25**	.00694	.00347	.00555
.00866	.00433	.00505	26	.00722	.00361	.00577
.00900	.00450	.00525	27	.00750	.00375	.00600
.00933	.00466	.00544	28	.00777	.00388	.00622
.00966	.00483	.00563	29	.00805	.00402	.00644
.01000	.00500	.00583	**30**	.00833	.00416	.00666
.01033	.00516	.00602	31	.00861	.00430	.00688
.01066	.00533	.00622	32	.00888	.00444	.00711
.01100	.00550	.00641	33	.00916	.00458	.00733

1 Dollar.

12 PER CENT.	6 PER CENT.	7 PER CENT.	DAYS.	10 PER CENT.	5 PER CENT.	8 PER CENT.
.01133	.00566	.00661	34	.00944	.00472	.00755
.01166	.00583	.00680	35	.00972	.00486	.00777
.01200	.00600	.00600	36	.01000	.00500	.00800
.01233	.00616	.00719	37	.01027	.00513	.00822
.01266	.00633	.00738	38	.01055	.00527	.00844
.01300	.00650	.00758	39	.01083	.00541	.00866
.01333	.00666	.00777	40	.01111	.00555	.00888
.01366	.00683	.00797	41	.01138	.00569	.00911
.01400	.00700	.00816	42	.01166	.00583	.00933
.01433	.00716	.00836	43	.01194	.00597	.00955
.01466	.00733	.00855	44	.01222	.00611	.00977
.01500	.00750	.00875	45	.01250	.00625	.01000
.01533	.00766	.00894	46	.01277	.00638	.01022
.01566	.00783	.00913	47	.01305	.00652	.01044
.01600	.00800	.00933	48	.01333	.00666	.01066
.01633	.00816	.00952	49	.01361	.00680	.01088
.01666	.00833	.00972	50	.01388	.00694	.01111
.01700	.00850	.00991	51	.01416	.00708	.01133
.01733	.00866	.01011	52	.01444	.00722	.01155
.01766	.00883	.01030	53	.01472	.00736	.01177
.01800	.00900	.01050	54	.01500	.00750	.01200
.01833	.00916	.01069	55	.01527	.00763	.01222
.01866	.00933	.01088	56	.01555	.00777	.01244
.01900	.00950	.01108	57	.01583	.00791	.01266
.01933	.00966	.01127	58	.01611	.00805	.01288
.01966	.00983	.01147	59	.01638	.00819	.01311
.02000	.01000	.01166	60	.01666	.00833	.01333
.02033	.01016	.01186	61	.01694	.00847	.01355
.02066	.01033	.01205	62	.01722	.00861	.01377
.02100	.01050	.01225	63	.01750	.00875	.01400
.02133	.01066	.01244	64	.01777	.00888	.01422
.02166	.01083	.01263	65	.01805	.00902	.01444
.02200	.01100	.01283	66	.01833	.00916	.01466
.02233	.01116	.01302	67	.01861	.00930	.01488
.02266	.01133	.01322	68	.01888	.00944	.01511
.02300	.01150	.01341	69	.01916	.00958	.01533
.02333	.01166	.01361	70	.01944	.00972	.01555
.02366	.01183	.01380	71	.01972	.00986	.01577
.02400	.01200	.01400	72	.02000	.01000	.01600
.02433	.01216	.01419	73	.02027	.01013	.01622
.02466	.01233	.01438	74	.02055	.01027	.01644
.02500	.01250	.01458	75	.02083	.01041	.01666
.02533	.01266	.01477	76	.02111	.01055	.01688
.02566	.01283	.01497	77	.02138	.01069	.01711
.02600	.01300	.01516	78	.02166	.01083	.01733
.02633	.01316	.01536	79	.02194	.01097	.01755
.02666	.01333	.01555	80	.02222	.01111	.01777
.02700	.01350	.01575	81	.02250	.01125	.01800
.02733	.01366	.01594	82	.02277	.01138	.01822
.02766	.01383	.01613	83	.02305	.01152	.01844
.02800	.01400	.01633	84	.02333	.01166	.01866

1 Dollar.

12 PER CENT.	6 PER CENT.	7 PER CENT.	DAYS.	10 PER CENT.	5 PER CENT.	8 PER CENT.
.02833	.01416	.01652	85	.02361	.01180	.01888
.02866	.01433	.01672	86	.02388	.01194	.01911
.02900	.01450	.01681	87	.02416	.01208	.01933
.02933	.01466	.01711	88	.02444	.01222	.01955
.02966	.01483	.01730	89	.02472	.01236	.01977
.03000	.01500	.01750	90	.02500	.01250	.02000
.03033	.01516	.01769	91	.02527	.01263	.02022
.03066	.01533	.01788	92	.02555	.01277	.02044
.03100	.01550	.01808	93	.02583	.01291	.02066
.03133	.01566	.01827	94	.02611	.01305	.02088
.03166	.01583	.01847	95	.02638	.01319	.02111
.03200	.01600	.01866	96	.02666	.01333	.02133
.03233	.01616	.01886	97	.02694	.01347	.02155
.03266	.01633	.01905	98	.02722	.01361	.02177
.03300	.01650	.01925	99	.02750	.01375	.02200
.03333	.01666	.01944	100	.02777	.01388	.02222

COMPOUND INTEREST TABLE.

TABLE III. (See Introduction.)

	3 Per Cent.	4 Per Cent.	4 1-2 Per Cent.	5 Per Cent.	6 Per Cent.	7 Per Cent.	8 Per Cent.
1	1.030000	1.040000	1.045000	1.050000	1.060000	1.070000	1.080000
2	1.060900	1.081600	1.092025	1.102500	1.123600	1.144900	1.166400
3	1.092727	1.124864	1.141166	1.157625	1.191016	1.225043	1.259712
4	1.125509	1.169859	1.192519	1.215506	1.262477	1.310796	1.360488
5	1.159274	1.216653	1.246182	1.276282	1.338226	1.402551	1.469328
6	1.194052	1.265319	1.302260	1.340096	1.418519	1.500730	1.586874
7	1.229874	1.315932	1.360862	1.407100	1.503630	1.605781	1.713824
8	1.266770	1.368569	1.422101	1.477455	1.593848	1.718186	1.850930
9	1.304773	1.423312	1.486095	1.551328	1.689479	1.838459	1.999004
10	1.343916	1.480244	1.552969	1.628895	1.790848	1.967151	2.158924
11	1.384234	1.539454	1.622853	1.710339	1.898299	2.104851	2.331638
12	1.425761	1.601032	1.695881	1.795856	2.012196	2.252191	2.518170
13	1.468534	1.665074	1.772196	1.885649	2.132928	2.409845	2.712623
14	1.512590	1.731676	1.851945	1.979932	2.260604	2.578534	2.937193
15	1.557967	1.800944	1.935282	2.078928	2.396558	2.759031	3.172169
16	1.604706	1.872981	2.022370	2.182875	2.540351	2.952163	3.425942
17	1.652848	1.947900	2.113376	2.292018	2.692773	3.158815	3.700018
18	1.702433	2.025817	2.208478	2.406619	2.854339	3.379932	3.996019
19	1.753506	2.106849	2.307860	2.526950	3.025600	3.616527	4.315701
20	1.806111	2.191123	2.411713	2.653298	3.107135	3.869684	4.660957

1 Dollar.

12 PER CENT.	6 PER CENT.	7 PER CENT.	YEARS.	10 PER CENT.	5 PER CENT.	8 PER CENT.
12	06	07	1	10	05	08
24	12	14	2	20	10	16
36	18	21	3	30	15	24
48	24	28	4	40	20	32
60	30	35	5	50	25	40
			MONTHS.			
01	01	01	1	01	0	01
02	01	01	2	02	01	01
03	02	02	3	03	01	02
04	02	02	4	03	02	03
05	03	03	5	04	02	03
06	03	04	**6**	05	03	04
07	04	04	7	06	03	05
08	04	05	8	07	03	05
09	05	05	9	08	04	06
10	05	06	10	08	04	07
11	06	06	11	09	05	07
			DAYS.			
0	0	0	1	0	0	0
0	0	0	2	0	0	0
0	0	0	3	0	0	0
0	0	0	4	0	0	0
0	0	0	**5**	0	0	0
0	0	0	6	0	0	0
0	0	0	7	0	0	0
0	0	0	8	0	0	0
0	0	0	9	0	0	0
0	0	0	**10**	0	0	0
0	0	0	11	0	0	0
0	0	0	12	0	0	0
0	0	0	13	0	0	0
0	0	0	14	0	0	0
01	0	0	**15**	0	0	0
01	0	0	16	0	0	0
01	0	0	17	0	0	0
01	0	0	18	01	0	0
01	0	0	19	01	0	0
01	0	0	**20**	01	0	0
01	0	0	21	01	0	0
01	0	0	22	01	0	0
01	0	0	23	01	0	01
01	0	0	24	01	0	01
01	0	0	**25**	01	0	01
01	0	01	26	01	0	01
01	0	01	27	01	0	01
01	0	01	28	01	0	01
01	0	01	29	01	0	01
01	01	01	**30**	01	0	01
01	01	01	33	01	0	01
02	01	01	63	02	01	02
03	02	02	93	03	01	03

2 Dollars.

12 PER CENT.	6 PER CENT.	7 PER CENT.	YEARS.	10 PER CENT.	5 PER CENT.	8 PER CENT.
24	12	14	1	20	10	16
48	24	28	2	40	20	32
72	36	42	3	60	30	48
96	48	56	4	80	40	64
1.20	60	70	5	1.00	50	80
			MONTHS.			
02	01	01	1	02	01	01
04	02	02	2	03	02	03
06	03	04	3	05	03	04
08	04	05	4	07	03	05
10	05	06	5	08	04	07
12	06	07	**6**	10	05	08
14	07	08	**7**	12	06	09
16	08	09	8	13	07	11
18	09	11	9	15	08	12
20	10	12	10	17	08	13
22	11	13	11	18	09	15
			DAYS.			
0	0	0	1	0	0	0
0	0	0	2	0	0	0
0	0	0	3	0	0	0
0	0	0	4	0	0	0
0	0	0	**5**	0	0	0
0	0	0	6	0	0	0
0	0	0	7	0	0	0
01	0	0	8	0	0	0
01	0	0	9	01	0	0
01	0	0	**10**	01	0	0
01	0	0	11	01	0	0
01	0	0	12	01	0	01
01	0	01	13	01	0	01
01	0	01	14	01	0	01
01	01	01	**15**	01	0	01
01	01	01	16	01	0	01
01	01	01	17	01	0	01
01	01	01	18	01	01	01
01	01	01	19	01	01	01
01	01	01	**20**	01	01	01
01	01	01	21	01	01	01
01	01	01	22	01	01	01
02	01	01	23	01	01	01
02	01	01	24	01	01	01
02	01	01	**25**	01	01	01
02	01	01	26	01	01	01
02	01	01	27	02	01	01
02	01	01	28	02	01	01
02	01	01	29	02	01	01
02	01	01	**30**	02	01	01
02	01	01	33	02	01	01
04	02	02	63	03	02	02
06	03	04	93	05	03	03

3 Dollars.

12 PER CENT.	6 PER CENT.	7 PER CENT.	YEARS.	10 PER CENT.	5 PER CENT.	8 PER CENT.
36	18	21	1	30	15	24
72	36	42	2	60	30	48
1.08	54	63	3	90	45	72
1.44	72	84	4	1.20	60	96
1.80	90	1.05	5	1.50	75	1.20
			MONTHS.			
03	02	02	1	03	01	02
06	03	04	2	05	03	04
09	05	05	3	08	04	06
12	06	07	4	10	05	08
15	08	09	5	13	06	10
18	09	11	**6**	15	08	12
21	11	12	7	18	09	14
24	12	14	8	20	10	16
27	14	16	9	23	11	18
30	15	18	10	25	13	20
33	17	19	11	28	14	22
			DAYS.			
0	0	0	1	0	0	0
0	0	0	2	0	0	0
0	0	0	3	0	0	0
0	0	0	4	0	0	0
01	0	0	**5**	0	0	0
01	0	0	6	01	0	0
01	0	0	7	01	0	0
01	0	0	8	01	0	01
01	0	01	9	01	0	01
01	01	01	**10**	01	0	01
01	01	01	11	01	0	01
01	01	01	12	01	01	01
01	01	01	13	01	01	01
01	01	01	14	01	01	01
02	01	01	**15**	01	01	01
02	01	01	16	01	01	01
02	01	01	17	01	01	01
02	01	01	18	02	01	01
02	01	01	19	02	01	01
02	01	01	**20**	02	01	01
02	01	01	21	02	01	01
02	01	01	22	02	01	01
02	01	01	23	02	01	02
02	01	01	24	02	01	02
03	01	01	**25**	02	01	02
03	01	02	26	02	01	02
03	01	02	27	02	01	02
03	01	02	28	02	01	02
03	01	02	29	02	01	02
03	02	02	**30**	03	01	02
03	02	02	33	03	01	02
06	03	04	63	05	03	04
09	05	05	93	08	04	06

4 Dollars.

12 PER CENT.	6 PER CENT.	7 PER CEMT.	YEARS.	10 PER CENT.	5 PER CENT	8 PER CENT
48	24	28	1	40	20	32
96	48	56	2	80	40	64
1.44	72	84	3	1.20	60	96
1.92	96	1.12	4	1.60	80	1.28
2.40	1.20	1.40	5	2.00	1.00	1.60
			MONTHS.			
04	02	02	1	03	02	03
08	04	05	2	07	03	05
12	06	07	3	10	05	08
16	08	09	4	13	07	11
20	10	12	5	17	08	13
24	12	14	**6**	20	10	16
28	14	16	7	23	12	19
32	16	19	8	27	13	21
36	18	21	9	30	15	24
40	20	23	10	33	17	27
44	22	26	11	37	18	29
			DAYS.			
0	0	0	1	0	0	0
0	0	0	2	0	0	0
0	0	0	3	0	0	0
01	0	0	4	0	0	0
01	0	0	**5**	01	0	0
01	0	0	6	01	0	01
01	0	01	7	01	0	01
01	01	01	8	01	0	01
01	01	01	9	01	01	01
01	01	01	**10**	01	01	01
01	01	01	11	01	01	01
02	01	01	12	01	01	01
02	01	01	13	01	01	01
02	01	01	14	02	01	01
02	01	01	**15**	02	01	01
02	01	01	16	02	01	01
02	01	01	17	02	01	02
02	01	01	18	02	01	02
03	01	01	19	02	01	02
03	01	02	**20**	02	01	02
03	01	02	21	02	01	02
03	01	02	22	02	01	02
03	02	02	23	03	01	02
03	02	02	24	03	01	02
03	02	02	**25**	03	01	02
03	02	02	26	03	01	02
04	02	02	27	03	02	02
04	02	02	28	03	02	02
04	02	02	29	03	02	03
04	02	02	**30**	03	02	03
04	02	02	33	04	02	03
08	04	05	63	07	03	06
12	06	07	93	10	05	08

5 Dollars.

12 PER CENT.	6 PER CENT.	7 PER CENT.	YEARS.	10 PER CENT.	5 PER CENT.	8 PER CENT.
60	30	35	1	50	25	40
1.20	60	70	2	1.00	50	80
1.80	90	1.05	3	1.50	75	1.20
2.40	1.20	1.40	4	2.00	1.00	1.60
3.00	1.50	1.75	5	2.50	1.25	2.00
			MONTHS.			
05	03	03	1	04	02	03
10	05	06	2	08	04	07
15	08	09	3	13	06	10
20	10	12	4	17	08	13
25	13	15	5	21	10	17
30	15	18	**6**	25	13	20
35	18	20	7	29	15	23
40	20	23	8	33	17	27
45	23	26	9	38	19	30
50	25	29	10	42	21	33
55	28	32	11	46	23	37
			DAYS.			
0	0	0	1	0	0	0
0	0	0	2	0	0	0
01	0	0	3	0	0	0
01	0	0	4	01	0	0
01	0	0	**5**	01	0	01
01	01	01	6	01	0	01
01	01	01	7	01	0	01
01	01	01	8	01	01	01
02	01	01	9	01	01	01
02	01	01	**10**	01	01	01
02	01	01	11	02	01	01
02	01	01	12	02	01	01
02	01	01	13	02	01	01
02	01	01	14	02	01	02
03	01	01	**15**	02	01	02
03	01	02	16	02	01	02
03	01	02	17	02	01	02
03	02	02	18	03	01	02
03	02	02	19	03	01	02
03	02	02	**20**	03	01	02
04	02	02	21	03	01	02
04	02	02	22	03	02	02
04	02	02	23	03	02	03
04	02	02	24	03	02	03
04	02	02	**25**	03	02	03
04	02	03	26	04	02	03
05	02	03	27	04	02	03
05	02	03	28	04	02	03
05	02	03	29	04	02	03
05	03	03	**30**	04	02	03
06	03	03	33	05	02	03
11	05	06	63	09	04	07
16	08	09	93	13	06	10

6 Dollars.

12 PER CENT.	6 PER CENT.	7 PER CENT.	YEARS.	10 PER CENT.	5 PER CENT.	8 PER CENT.
72	36	42	1	60	30	48
1.44	72	84	2	1.20	60	96
2.16	1.08	1.26	3	1.80	90	1.44
2.88	1.44	1.68	4	2.40	1.20	1.92
3.60	1.80	2.10	5	3.00	1.50	2.40
			MONTHS.			
06	03	04	1	05	03	04
12	06	07	2	10	05	08
18	09	11	3	15	08	12
24	12	14	4	20	10	16
30	15	18	5	25	13	20
36	18	21	**6**	30	15	24
42	21	25	7	35	18	28
48	24	28	8	40	20	32
54	27	32	9	45	23	36
60	30	35	10	50	25	40
66	33	39	11	55	28	44
			DAYS.			
0	0	0	1	0	0	0
0	0	0	2	0	0	0
01	0	0	3	01	0	0
01	0	0	4	01	0	01
01	01	01	**5**	01	0	01
01	01	01	6	01	01	01
01	01	01	7	01	01	01
02	01	01	8	01	01	01
02	01	01	9	02	01	01
02	01	01	**10**	02	01	01
02	01	01	11	02	01	01
02	01	01	12	02	01	02
03	01	02	13	02	01	02
03	01	02	14	02	01	02
03	02	02	**15**	03	01	02
03	02	02	16	03	01	02
03	02	02	17	03	01	02
04	02	02	18	03	02	02
04	02	02	19	03	02	03
04	02	02	**20**	03	02	03
04	02	02	21	04	02	03
04	02	03	22	04	02	03
05	02	03	23	04	02	03
05	02	03	24	04	02	03
05	03	03	**25**	04	02	03
05	03	03	26	04	02	03
05	03	03	27	05	02	04
06	03	03	28	05	02	04
06	03	03	29	05	02	04
06	03	04	**30**	05	03	04
07	03	04	33	06	03	04
13	06	07	63	11	05	08
19	09	11	93	16	08	12

7 Dollars.

12 PER CENT.	6 PER CENT.	7 PER CENT.	YEARS.	10 PER CENT.	5 PER CENT.	8 PER CENT.
84	42	49	1	70	35	56
1.68	84	98	2	1.40	70	1.12
2.52	1.26	1.47	3	2.10	1.05	1.68
3.36	1.68	1.96	4	2.80	1.40	2.24
4.20	2.10	2.45	5	3.50	1.75	2.80
			MONTHS.			
07	04	04	1	06	03	05
14	07	08	2	12	06	09
21	11	12	3	18	09	14
28	14	16	4	23	12	19
35	18	20	5	29	15	23
42	21	25	**6**	35	18	28
49	25	29	7	41	20	33
56	28	33	8	47	23	37
63	32	37	9	53	26	42
70	35	41	10	58	29	47
77	39	45	11	64	32	51
			DAYS.			
0	0	0	1	0	0	0
0	0	0	2	0	0	0
01	0	0	3	01	0	0
01	0	01	4	01	0	01
01	01	01	**5**	01	0	01
01	01	01	6	01	01	01
02	01	01	7	01	01	01
02	01	01	8	02	01	01
02	01	01	9	02	01	01
02	01	01	**10**	02	01	02
03	01	01	11	02	01	02
03	01	02	12	02	01	02
03	02	02	13	03	01	02
03	02	02	14	03	01	02
04	02	02	**15**	03	01	02
04	02	02	16	03	02	02
04	02	02	17	03	02	03
04	02	02	18	04	02	03
04	02	03	19	04	02	03
05	02	03	**20**	04	02	03
05	02	03	21	04	02	03
05	03	03	22	04	02	03
05	03	03	23	04	02	04
06	03	03	24	05	02	04
06	03	03	**25**	05	02	04
06	03	04	26	05	03	04
06	03	04	27	05	03	04
07	03	04	28	05	03	04
07	03	04	29	06	03	05
07	04	04	**30**	06	03	05
08	04	04	33	06	03	05
15	07	09	63	12	06	10
22	11	13	93	18	09	14

8 Dollars.

12 PER CENT.	6 PER CENT.	7 PER CENT.	YEARS.	10 PER CENT.	5 PER CENT.	8 PER CENT.
96	48	56	1	80	40	64
1.92	96	1.12	2	1.60	80	1.28
2.88	1.44	1.68	3	2.40	1.20	1.92
3.84	1.92	2.24	4	3.20	1.60	2.56
4.80	2.40	2.80	5	4.00	2.00	3.20
			MONTHS.			
08	04	05	1	07	03	05
16	08	09	2	13	07	11
24	12	14	3	20	10	16
32	16	19	4	27	13	21
40	20	23	5	33	17	27
48	24	28	**6**	40	20	32
56	28	33	7	47	23	37
64	32	37	8	53	27	43
72	36	42	9	60	30	48
80	40	47	10	67	33	53
88	44	51	11	73	37	59
			DAYS.			
0	0	0	1	0	0	0
01	0	0	2	0	0	0
01	0	0	3	01	0	01
01	01	01	4	01	0	01
01	01	01	**5**	01	01	01
02	01	01	6	01	01	01
02	01	01	7	02	01	01
02	01	01	8	02	01	01
02	01	01	9	02	01	02
03	01	02	**10**	02	01	02
03	01	02	11	02	01	02
03	02	02	12	03	01	02
03	02	02	13	03	01	02
04	02	02	14	03	02	02
04	02	02	**15**	03	02	03
04	02	02	16	04	02	03
05	02	03	17	04	02	03
05	02	03	18	04	02	03
05	03	03	19	04	02	03
05	03	03	**20**	04	02	04
06	03	03	21	05	02	04
06	03	03	22	05	02	04
06	03	04	23	05	03	04
06	03	04	24	05	03	04
07	03	04	**25**	06	03	04
07	03	04	26	06	03	05
07	04	04	27	06	03	05
07	04	04	28	06	03	05
08	04	05	29	06	03	05
08	04	05	**30**	07	03	05
09	04	05	33	07	04	06
17	08	10	63	14	07	11
25	12	14	93	21	10	16

9 Dollars.

12 PER CENT.	6 PER CENT.	7 PER CENT.	YEARS.	10 PER CENT.	5 PER CENT.	8 PER CENT.
1.08	54	63	1	90	45	72
2.16	1.08	1.26	2	1.80	90	1.44
3.24	1.62	1.89	3	2.70	1.35	2.16
4.32	2.16	2.52	4	3.60	1.80	2.88
5.40	2.70	3.15	5	4.50	2.25	3.60
			MONTHS.			
09	05	05	1	08	04	06
18	09	11	2	15	08	12
27	14	16	3	23	11	18
36	18	21	4	30	15	24
45	23	26	**5**	38	19	30
54	27	32	**6**	45	23	36
63	32	37	**7**	53	26	42
72	36	42	8	60	30	48
81	41	47	9	68	34	54
90	45	53	10	75	38	60
99	50	58	11	83	41	66
			DAYS.			
0	0	0	1	0	0	0
01	0	0	2	01	0	0
01	0	01	3	01	0	01
01	01	01	4	01	01	01
02	01	01	**5**	01	01	01
02	01	01	6	02	01	01
02	01	01	7	02	01	01
02	01	01	8	02	01	02
03	01	02	9	02	01	02
03	02	02	**10**	03	01	02
03	02	02	11	03	01	02
04	02	02	12	03	02	02
04	02	02	13	03	02	03
04	02	02	14	04	02	03
05	02	03	**15**	04	02	03
05	02	03	16	04	02	03
05	03	03	17	04	02	03
05	03	03	18	05	02	04
06	03	03	19	05	02	04
06	03	04	**20**	05	03	04
06	03	04	21	05	03	04
07	03	04	22	06	03	04
07	03	04	23	06	03	05
07	04	04	24	06	03	05
08	04	04	**25**	06	03	05
08	04	05	26	07	03	05
08	04	05	27	07	03	05
08	04	05	28	07	04	06
09	04	05	29	07	04	06
09	05	05	**30**	08	04	06
10	05	06	33	08	04	07
19	09	11	63	16	08	13
28	14	16	93	23	12	19

10 Dollars.

12 PER CENT.	6 PER CENT.	7 PER CENT.	YEARS.	10 PER CENT.	5 PER CENT.	8 PER CENT.
1.20	60	70	1	1.00	50	80
2.40	1.20	1.40	2	2.00	1.00	1.60
3.60	1.80	2.10	3	3.00	1.50	2.40
4.80	2.40	2.80	4	4.00	2.00	3.20
6.00	3:00	3.50	5	5.00	2.50	4.00
			MONTHS.			
10	05	06	1	08	04	07
20	10	12	2	17	08	13
30	15	18	3	25	13	20
40	20	23	4	33	17	27
50	25	29	5	42	21	33
60	30	35	**6**	50	25	40
70	35	41	7	58	29	47
80	40	47	8	67	33	53
90	45	53	9	75	38	60
1.00	50	58	10	83	42	67
1.10	55	64	11	92	46	73
			DAYS.			
0	0	0	1	0	0	0
01	0	0	2	01	0	0
01	01	01	3	01	0	01
01	01	01	4	01	01	01
02	01	01	**5**	01	01	01
02	01	01	6	02	01	01
02	01	01	7	02	01	02
03	01	02	8	02	01	02
03	02	02	9	03	01	02
03	02	02	**10**	03	01	02
04	02	02	11	03	02	02
04	02	02	12	03	02	03
04	02	03	13	04	02	03
05	02	03	14	04	02	03
05	03	03	**15**	04	02	03
05	03	03	16	04	02	04
06	03	03	17	05	02	04
06	03	04	18	05	03	04
06	03	04	19	05	03	04
07	03	04	**20**	06	03	04
07	04	04	21	06	03	05
07	04	04	22	06	03	05
08	04	04	23	06	03	05
08	04	05	24	07	03	05
08	04	05	**25**	07	03	06
09	04	05	26	07	04	06
09	05	05	27	08	04	06
09	05	05	28	08	04	06
10	05	06	29	08	04	06
10	05	06	**30**	08	04	07
11	06	06	33	09	05	07
21	11	12	63	18	09	14
31	16	18	93	26	13	21

11 Dollars.

12 PER CENT.	6 PER CENT.	7 PER CENT.	YEARS.	10 PER CENT.	5 PER CENT.	8 PER CENT.
1.32	66	77	1	1.10	55	88
2.64	1.32	1.54	2	2.20	1.10	1.76
3.96	1.98	2.31	3	3.30	1.65	2.64
5.28	2.64	3.08	4	4.40	2.20	3.52
6.60	3.30	3.85	5	5.50	2.75	4.40
			MONTHS.			
11	06	06	1	09	05	07
22	11	13	2	18	09	15
33	17	19	3	28	14	22
44	22	26	4	37	18	29
55	28	32	5	46	23	37
66	33	39	**6**	55	28	44
77	39	45	7	64	32	51
88	44	51	8	73	37	59
99	50	58	9	83	41	66
1.10	55	64	10	92	46	73
1.21	61	71	11	1.01	50	81
			DAYS.			
0	0	0	1	0	0	0
01	0	0	2	01	0	0
01	01	01	3	01	0	01
01	01	01	4	01	01	01
02	01	01	**5**	02	01	01
02	01	01	6	02	01	01
03	01	01	7	02	01	02
03	01	02	8	02	01	02
03	02	02	9	03	01	02
04	02	02	**10**	03	02	02
04	02	02	11	03	02	03
04	02	03	12	04	02	03
05	02	03	13	04	02	03
05	03	03	14	04	02	03
06	03	03	**15**	05	02	04
06	03	03	16	05	02	04
06	03	04	17	05	03	04
07	03	04	18	06	03	04
07	03	04	19	06	03	05
07	04	04	**20**	06	03	05
08	04	04	21	06	03	05
08	04	05	22	07	03	05
08	04	05	23	07	04	06
09	04	05	24	07	04	06
09	05	05	**25**	08	04	06
10	05	06	26	08	04	06
10	05	06	27	08	04	07
10	05	06	28	09	04	07
11	05	06	29	09	04	07
11	06	06	**30**	09	05	07
12	06	07	33	10	05	08
23	12	13	63	19	10	15
34	17	20	93	28	14	23

12 Dollars.

12 PER CENT.	6 PER CENT.	7 PER CENT.	YEARS.	10 PER CENT.	5 PER CENT.	8 PER CENT.
1.44	72	84	1	1.20	60	96
2.88	1.44	1.68	2	2.40	1.20	1.92
4.32	2.16	2.52	3	3.60	1.80	2.88
5.76	2.88	3.36	4	4.80	2.40	3.84
7.20	3.60	4.20	5	6.00	3.00	4.80
			MONTHS.			
12	06	07	1	10	05	08
24	12	14	2	20	10	16
36	18	21	3	30	15	24
48	24	28	4	40	20	32
60	30	35	5	50	25	40
72	36	42	**6**	60	30	48
84	42	49	7	70	35	56
96	48	56	8	80	40	64
1.08	54	63	9	90	45	72
1.20	60	70	10	1.00	50	80
1.32	66	77	11	1.10	55	88
			DAYS.			
0	0	0	1	0	0	0
01	0	0	2	01	0	01
01	01	01	3	01	01	01
02	01	01	4	01	01	01
02	01	01	**5**	02	01	01
02	01	01	6	02	01	02
03	01	02	7	02	01	02
03	02	02	8	03	01	02
04	02	02	9	03	02	02
04	02	02	**10**	03	02	03
04	02	03	11	04	02	03
05	02	03	12	04	02	03
05	03	03	13	04	02	03
06	03	03	14	05	02	04
06	03	04	**15**	05	03	04
06	03	04	16	05	03	04
07	03	04	17	06	03	05
07	04	04	18	06	03	05
08	04	04	19	06	03	05
08	04	05	**20**	07	03	05
08	04	05	21	07	04	06
09	04	05	22	07	04	06
09	05	05	23	08	04	06
10	05	06	24	08	04	06
10	05	06	**25**	08	04	07
10	05	06	26	09	04	07
11	05	06	27	09	05	07
11	06	07	28	09	05	07
12	06	07	29	10	05	08
12	06	07	**30**	10	05	08
13	07	08	33	11	06	09
25	13	15	63	21	11	17
37	19	22	93	31	16	25

13 Dollars.

12 PER CENT.	6 PER CENT.	7 PER CENT.	YEARS.	10 PER CENT.	5 PER CENT.	8 PER CENT.
1.56	78	91	1	1.30	65	1.04
3.12	1.56	1.82	2	2.60	1.30	2.08
4.68	2.34	2.73	3	3.90	1.95	3.12
6.24	3.12	3.64	4	5.20	2.60	4.16
7.80	3.90	4.55	5	6.50	3.25	5.20
			MONTHS.			
13	07	08	1	11	05	09
26	13	15	2	22	11	17
39	20	23	3	33	16	26
52	26	30	4	43	22	35
65	33	38	5	54	27	43
78	39	46	**6**	65	33	52
91	46	53	7	76	38	61
1.04	52	61	8	87	43	69
1.17	59	68	9	98	49	78
1.30	65	76	10	1.08	54	87
1.43	72	83	11	1.19	60	95
			DAYS.			
0	0	0	1	0	0	0
01	0	0	2	01	0	01
01	01	01	3	01	01	01
02	01	01	4	01	01	01
02	01	01	**5**	02	01	01
03	01	02	6	02	01	02
03	02	02	7	03	01	02
03	02	02	8	03	01	02
04	02	02	9	03	02	03
04	02	03	**10**	04	02	03
05	02	03	11	04	02	03
05	03	03	12	04	02	03
06	03	03	13	05	02	04
06	03	04	14	05	03	04
07	03	04	**15**	05	03	04
07	03	04	16	06	03	05
07	04	04	17	06	03	05
08	04	05	18	07	03	05
08	04	05	19	07	03	05
09	04	05	**20**	07	04	06
09	05	05	21	08	04	06
10	05	06	22	08	04	06
10	05	06	23	08	04	07
10	05	06	24	09	04	07
11	05	06	**25**	09	05	07
11	06	07	26	09	05	08
12	06	07	27	10	05	08
12	06	07	28	10	05	08
13	06	07	29	10	05	08
13	07	08	**30**	11	05	09
14	07	08	33	12	06	09
27	14	16	63	23	11	18
40	20	24	93	34	17	27

14 Dollars.

12 PER CENT.	6 PER CENT.	7 PER CENT.	YEARS.	10 PER CENT.	5 PER CENT.	8 PER CENT.
1.68	84	98	1	1.40	70	1.12
3.36	1.68	1.96	2	2.80	1.40	2.24
5.04	2.52	2.94	3	4.20	2.10	3.36
6.72	3.36	3.92	4	5.60	2.80	4.48
8.40	4.20	4.90	5	7.00	3.50	5.60
			MONTHS.			
14	07	08	1	12	06	09
28	14	16	2	23	12	19
42	21	25	3	35	18	28
56	28	33	4	47	23	37
70	35	41	5	58	29	47
84	42	49	**6**	70	35	56
98	49	57	7	82	41	65
1.12	56	65	8	93	47	75
1.26	63	74	9	1.05	53	84
1.40	70	82	10	1.17	58	93
1.54	77	90	11	1.28	64	1.03
			DAYS.			
0	0	0	1	0	0	0
01	0	01	2	01	0	01
01	01	01	3	01	01	01
02	01	01	4	02	01	01
02	01	01	**5**	02	01	02
03	01	02	6	02	01	02
03	02	02	7	03	01	02
04	02	02	8	03	02	02
04	02	02	9	04	02	03
05	02	03	**10**	04	02	03
05	03	03	11	04	02	03
06	03	03	12	05	02	04
06	03	04	13	05	03	04
07	03	04	14	05	03	04
07	04	04	**15**	06	03	05
07	04	04	16	06	03	05
08	04	05	17	07	03	05
08	04	05	18	07	04	06
09	04	05	19	07	04	06
09	05	05	**20**	08	04	06
10	05	06	21	08	04	07
10	05	06	22	09	04	07
11	05	06	23	09	04	07
11	06	07	24	09	05	07
12	06	07	**25**	10	05	08
12	06	07	26	10	05	08
13	06	07	27	11	05	08
13	07	08	28	11	05	09
14	07	08	29	11	06	09
14	07	08	**30**	12	06	09
15	08	09	33	13	06	10
29	15	17	63	25	12	20
43	22	25	93	36	18	29

15 Dollars.

12 PER CENT.	6 PER CENT.	7 PER CENT.	YEARS.	10 PER CENT.	5 PER CENT.	8 PER CENT.
1.80	90	1.05	1	1.50	75	1.20
3.60	1.80	2.10	2	3.00	1.50	2.40
5.40	2.70	3.15	3	4.50	2.25	3.60
7.20	3.60	4.20	4	6.00	3.00	4.80
9.00	4.50	5.25	5	7.50	3.75	6.00
			MONTHS.			
15	08	09	1	13	06	10
30	15	18	2	25	13	20
45	23	26	3	38	19	30
60	30	35	4	50	25	40
75	38	44	5	63	31	50
90	45	53	**6**	75	38	60
1.05	53	61	7	88	44	70
1.20	60	70	8	1.00	50	80
1.35	68	79	9	1.13	56	90
1.50	75	88	10	1.25	63	1.00
1.65	83	96	11	1.38	69	1.10
			DAYS.			
01	0	0	1	0	0	0
01	01	01	2	01	0	01
02	01	01	3	01	01	01
02	01	01	4	02	01	01
03	01	01	**5**	02	01	02
03	02	02	6	03	01	02
04	02	02	7	03	01	02
04	02	02	8	03	02	03
05	02	03	9	04	02	03
05	03	03	**10**	04	02	03
06	03	03	11	05	02	04
06	03	04	12	05	03	04
07	03	04	13	05	03	04
07	04	04	14	06	03	05
08	04	04	**15**	06	03	05
08	04	05	16	07	03	05
09	04	05	17	07	04	06
09	05	05	18	08	04	06
10	05	06	19	08	04	06
10	05	06	**20**	08	04	07
11	05	06	21	09	04	07
11	06	06	22	09	05	07
12	06	07	23	10	05	08
12	06	07	24	10	05	08
13	06	07	**25**	10	05	08
13	07	08	26	11	05	09
14	07	08	27	11	06	09
14	07	08	28	12	06	09
15	07	08	29	12	06	10
15	08	09	**30**	13	06	10
17	08	10	33	14	07	11
32	16	18	63	26	13	21
47	23	27	93	39	19	31

16 Dollars.

12 PER CENT.	6 PER CENT.	7 PER CENT.	YEARS.	10 PER CENT.	5 PER CENT.	8 PER CENT.
1.92	96	1.12	1	1.60	80	1.28
3.84	1.92	2.24	2	3.20	1.60	2.56
5.76	2.88	3.36	3	4.80	2.40	3.84
7.68	3.84	4.48	4	6.40	3.20	5.12
9.60	4.80	5.60	5	8.00	4.00	6.40
			MONTHS.			
16	08	09	1	13	07	11
32	16	19	2	27	13	21
48	24	28	3	40	20	32
64	32	37	4	53	27	43
80	40	47	5	67	33	53
96	48	56	**6**	80	40	64
1.12	56	65	7	93	47	75
1.28	64	75	8	1.07	53	85
1.44	72	84	9	1.20	60	96
1.60	80	93	10	1.33	67	1.07
1.76	88	1.03	11	1.47	73	1.17
			DAYS.			
01	0	0	1	0	0	0
01	01	01	2	01	0	01
02	01	01	3	01	01	01
02	01	01	4	02	01	01
03	01	02	**5**	02	01	02
03	02	02	6	03	01	02
04	02	02	7	03	02	02
04	02	02	8	04	02	03
05	02	03	9	04	02	03
05	03	03	**10**	04	02	04
06	03	03	11	05	02	04
06	03	04	12	05	03	04
07	03	04	13	06	03	05
07	04	04	14	06	03	05
08	04	05	**15**	07	03	05
09	04	05	16	07	04	06
09	05	05	17	08	04	06
10	05	06	18	08	04	06
10	05	06	19	08	04	07
11	05	06	**20**	09	04	07
11	06	07	21	09	05	07
12	06	07	22	10	05	08
12	06	07	23	10	05	08
13	06	07	24	11	05	09
13	07	08	**25**	11	06	09
14	07	08	26	12	06	09
14	07	08	27	12	06	10
15	07	09	28	12	06	10
15	08	09	29	13	06	10
16	08	09	**30**	13	07	11
18	09	10	33	15	07	12
34	17	20	63	28	14	22
50	25	29	93	41	21	33

17 Dollars.

12 PER CENT.	6 PER CENT.	7 PER CENT.	YEARS.	10 PER CENT.	5 PER CENT.	8 PER CENT.
2.04	1.02	1.19	1	1.70	85	1.36
4.08	2.04	2.38	2	3.40	1.70	2.72
6.12	3.06	3.57	3	5.10	2.55	4.08
8.16	4.08	4.76	4	6.80	3.40	5.44
10.20	5.10	5.95	5	8.50	4.25	6.80
			MONTHS.			
.17	09	10	1	14	07	11
34	17	20	2	28	14	23
51	26	30	3	43	21	34
68	34	40	4	57	28	45
85	43	50	5	71	35	57
1.02	51	60	**6**	85	43	68
1.19	60	69	7	99	50	79
1.36	68	79	8	1.13	57	91
1.53	77	89	9	1.28	64	1.02
1.70	85	99	10	1.42	71	1.13
1.87	94	1.09	11	1.56	78	1.25
			DAYS.			
01	0	0	1	0	0	0
01	01	01	2	01	0	01
02	01	01	3	01	01	01
02	01	01	4	02	01	02
03	01	02	**5**	02	01	02
03	02	02	6	03	01	02
04	02	02	7	03	02	03
05	02	03	8	04	02	03
05	03	03	9	04	02	03
06	03	03	**10**	05	02	04
06	03	04	11	05	03	04
07	03	04	12	06	03	05
07	04	04	13	06	03	05
08	04	05	14	07	03	05
09	04	05	**15**	07	04	06
09	05	05	16	08	04	06
10	05	06	17	08	04	06
10	05	06	18	09	04	07
11	05	06	19	09	04	07
11	06	07	**20**	09	05	08
12	06	07	21	10	05	08
12	06	07	22	10	05	08
13	07	08	23	11	05	09
14	07	08	24	11	06	09
14	07	08	**25**	12	06	09
15	07	09	26	12	06	10
15	08	09	27	13	06	10
16	08	09	28	13	07	11
16	08	10	29	14	07	11
17	09	10	**30**	14	07	11
19	09	11	33	16	08	12
36	18	21	63	30	15	23
53	26	31	93	44	22	35

18 Dollars.

12 PER CENT.	6 PER CENT.	7 PER CENT.	YEARS.	10 PER CENT.	5 PER CENT.	8 PER CENT.
2.16	1.08	1.26	1	1.80	90	1.44
4.32	2.16	2.52	2	3.60	1.80	2.88
6.48	3.24	3.78	3	5.40	2.70	4.32
8.64	4.32	5.04	4	7.20	3.60	5.76
10.80	5.40	6.30	5	9.00	4.50	7.20
			MONTHS.			
18	09	11	1	15	08	12
36	18	21	2	30	15	24
54	27	32	3	45	23	36
72	36	42	4	60	30	48
90	45	53	5	75	38	60
1.08	54	63	**6**	90	45	72
1.26	63	74	7	1.05	53	84
1.44	72	84	8	1.20	60	96
1.62	81	95	9	1.35	68	1.08
1.80	90	1.05	10	1.50	75	1.20
1.98	99	1.16	11	1.65	83	1.32
			DAYS.			
01	0	0	1	01	0	0
01	01	01	2	01	01	01
02	01	01	3	02	01	01
02	01	01	4	02	01	02
03	02	02	**5**	03	01	02
04	02	02	6	03	02	02
04	02	02	7	04	02	03
05	02	03	8	04	02	03
05	03	03	9	05	02	04
06	03	04	**10**	05	03	04
07	03	04	11	06	03	04
07	04	04	12	06	03	05
08	04	05	13	07	03	05
08	04	05	14	07	04	06
09	05	05	**15**	08	04	06
10	05	06	16	08	04	06
10	05	06	17	09	04	07
11	05	06	18	09	05	07
11	06	07	19	10	05	08
12	06	07	**20**	10	05	08
13	06	07	21	11	05	08
13	07	08	22	11	06	09
14	07	08	23	12	06	09
14	07	08	24	12	06	10
15	08	09	**25**	13	06	10
16	08	09	26	13	07	10
16	08	09	27	14	07	11
17	08	10	28	14	07	11
17	09	10	29	15	07	12
18	09	11	**30**	15	08	12
20	10	12	33	17	08	13
38	19	22	63	32	16	25
56	28	33	93	47	23	37

19 Dollars.

12 PER CENT.	6 PER CENT.	7 PER CENT.	YEARS.	10 PER CENT.	5 PER CENT.	8 PER CENT.
2.28	1.14	1.33	1	1.90	95	1.52
4.56	2.28	2.66	2	3.80	1.90	3.04
6.84	3.42	3.99	3	5.70	2.85	4.56
9.12	4.56	5.32	4	7.60	3.80	6.08
11.40	5.70	6.65	5	9.50	4.75	7.60
			MONTHS.			
19	10	11	1	16	08	13
38	19	22	2	32	16	25
57	29	33	3	48	24	38
76	38	44	4	63	32	51
95	48	55	5	79	40	63
1.14	57	67	**6**	95	48	76
1.33	67	78	7	1.11	55	89
1.52	76	89	8	1.27	63	1.01
1.71	86	1.00	9	1.43	71	1.14
1.90	95	1.11	10	1.58	79	1.27
2.09	1.05	1.22	11	1.74	87	1.39
			DAYS.			
01	0	0	1	01	0	0
01	01	01	2	01	01	01
02	01	01	3	02	01	01
03	01	01	4	02	01	02
03	02	02	**5**	03	01	02
04	02	02	6	03	02	03
04	02	03	7	04	02	03
05	03	03	8	04	02	03
06	03	03	9	05	02	04
06	03	04	**10**	05	03	04
07	03	04	11	06	03	05
08	04	04	12	06	03	05
08	04	05	13	07	03	05
09	04	05	14	07	04	06
10	05	06	**15**	08	04	06
10	05	06	16	08	04	07
11	05	06	17	09	04	07
11	06	07	18	10	05	08
12	06	07	19	10	05	08
13	06	07	**20**	11	05	08
13	07	08	21	11	06	09
14	07	08	22	12	06	09
15	07	08	23	12	06	10
15	08	09	24	13	06	10
16	08	09	**25**	13	07	11
16	08	10	26	14	07	11
17	09	10	27	14	07	11
18	09	10	28	15	07	12
18	09	11	29	15	08	12
19	10	11	**30**	16	08	13
21	10	12	33	17	09	14
40	20	23	63	33	17	27
59	29	34	93	49	25	40

20 Dollars.

12 PER CENT.	6 PER CENT.	7 PER CENT.	YEARS.	10 PER CENT.	5 PER CENT.	8 PER CENT.
2.40	1.20	1.40	1	2.00	1.00	1.60
4.80	2.40	2.80	2	4.00	2.00	3.20
7.20	3.60	4.20	3	6.00	3.00	4.80
9.60	4.80	5.60	4	8.00	4.00	6.40
12.00	6.00	7.00	5	10.00	5.00	8.00
			MONTHS.			
20	10	12	1	17	08	13
40	20	23	2	33	17	27
60	30	35	3	50	25	40
80	40	47	4	67	33	53
1.00	50	58	5	83	42	67
1.20	60	70	**6**	1.00	50	80
1.40	70	82	7	1.17	58	93
1.60	80	93	8	1.33	67	1.07
1.80	90	1.05	9	1.50	75	1.20
2.00	1.00	1.17	10	1.67	83	1.33
2.20	1.10	1.28	11	1.83	92	1.47
			DAYS.			
01	0	0	1	01	0	0
01	01	01	2	01	01	01
02	01	01	3	02	01	01
03	01	02	4	02	01	02
03	02	02	**5**	03	01	02
04	02	02	6	03	02	03
05	02	03	7	04	02	03
05	03	03	8	04	02	04
06	03	04	9	05	03	04
07	03	04	**10**	06	03	04
07	04	04	11	06	03	05
08	04	05	12	07	03	05
09	04	05	13	07	04	06
09	05	05	14	08	04	06
10	05	06	**15**	08	04	07
11	05	06	16	09	04	07
11	06	07	17	09	05	08
12	06	07	18	10	05	08
13	06	07	19	11	05	08
13	07	08	**20**	11	06	09
14	07	08	21	12	06	09
15	07	09	22	12	06	10
15	08	09	23	13	06	10
16	08	09	24	13	07	11
17	08	10	**25**	14	07	11
17	09	10	26	14	07	12
18	09	11	27	15	08	12
19	09	11	28	16	08	12
19	10	11	29	16	08	13
20	10	12	**30**	17	08	13
22	11	13	33	18	09	14
42	21	25	63	35	18	28
62	31	36	93	52	26	40

21 Dollars.

12 PER CENT.	6 PER CENT.	7 PER CENT.	YEARS.	10 PER CENT.	5 PER CENT.	8 PER CENT.
2.52	1.26	1.47	1	2.10	1.05	1.68
5.04	2.52	2.94	2	4.20	2.10	3.36
7.56	3.78	4.41	3	6.30	3.15	5.04
10.08	5.04	5.88	4	8.40	4.20	6.72
12.60	6.30	7.35	5	10.50	5.25	8.40
			MONTHS.			
21	11	12	1	18	09	14
42	21	25	2	35	18	28
63	32	37	3	53	26	42
84	42	49	4	70	35	56
1.05	53	61	5	88	44	70
1.26	63	74	**6**	1.05	53	84
1.47	74	86	7	1.23	61	98
1.68	84	98	8	1.40	70	1.12
1.89	95	1.10	9	1.58	79	1.26
2.10	1.05	1.23	10	1.75	88	1.40
2.31	1.16	1.35	11	1.93	96	1.54
			DAYS.			
01	0	0	1	01	0	0
01	01	01	2	01	01	01
02	01	01	3	02	01	01
03	01	02	4	02	01	02
04	02	02	**5**	03	01	02
04	02	02	6	04	02	03
05	02	03	7	04	02	03
06	03	03	8	05	02	04
06	03	04	9	05	03	04
07	04	04	**10**	06	03	05
08	04	04	11	06	03	05
08	04	05	12	07	04	06
09	05	05	13	08	04	06
10	05	06	14	08	04	07
11	05	06	**15**	09	04	07
11	06	07	16	09	05	07
12	06	07	17	10	05	08
13	06	07	18	11	05	08
13	07	08	19	11	06	09
14	07	08	**20**	12	06	09
15	07	09	21	12	06	10
15	08	09	22	13	06	10
16	08	09	23	13	07	11
17	08	10	24	14	07	11
18	09	10	**25**	15	07	12
18	09	11	26	15	08	12
19	09	11	27	16	08	13
20	10	11	28	16	08	13
20	10	12	29	17	08	14
21	11	12	**30**	18	09	14
23	12	13	33	19	10	15
44	22	26	63	37	18	29
65	33	38	93	54	27	43

22 Dollars.

12 PER CENT.	6 PER CENT.	7 PER CENT.	YEARS.	10 PER CENT.	5 PER CENT.	8 PER CENT.
2.64	1.32	1.54	1	2.20	1.10	1.76
5.28	2.64	3.08	2	4.40	2.20	3.52
7.92	3.96	4.62	3	6.60	3.30	5.28
10.56	5.28	6.16	4	8.80	4.40	7.04
13.20	6.60	7.70	5	11.00	5.50	8.80
			MONTHS.			
22	11	13	1	18	09	15
44	22	26	2	37	18	29
66	33	39	3	55	28	44
88	44	51	4	73	37	59
1.10	55	64	5	92	46	73
1.32	66	77	**6**	1.10	55	88
1.54	77	90	7	1.28	64	1.03
1.76	88	1.03	8	1.47	73	1.17
1.98	99	1.16	9	1.65	83	1.32
2.20	1.10	1.28	10	1.83	92	1.47
2.42	1.21	1.41	11	2.02	1.01	1.61
			DAYS.			
01	0	0	1	01	0	0
01	01	01	2	01	01	01
02	01	01	3	02	01	01
03	01	02	4	02	01	02
04	02	02	**5**	03	02	02
04	02	03	6	04	02	03
05	03	03	7	04	02	03
06	03	03	8	05	02	04
07	03	04	9	06	03	04
07	04	04	**10**	06	03	05
08	04	05	11	07	03	05
09	04	05	12	07	04	06
10	05	06	13	08	04	06
10	05	06	14	09	04	07
11	06	06	**15**	09	05	07
12	06	07	16	10	05	08
12	06	07	17	10	05	08
13	07	08	18	11	06	09
14	07	08	19	12	06	09
15	07	09	**20**	12	06	10
15	08	09	21	13	06	10
16	08	09	22	13	07	11
17	08	10	23	14	07	11
18	09	10	24	15	07	12
18	09	11	**25**	15	08	12
19	10	11	26	16	08	13
20	10	12	27	17	08	13
21	10	12	28	17	09	14
21	11	12	29	18	09	14
22	11	13	**30**	18	09	15
24	12	14	33	20	10	16
46	23	27	63	38	19	31
68	34	40	93	57	28	46

23 Dollars.

12 PER CENT.	6 PER CENT.	7 PER CENT.	YEARS.	10 PER CENT.	5 PER CENT.	8 PER CENT.
2.76	1.38	1.61	1	2.30	1.15	1.84
5.52	2.76	3.22	2	4.60	2.30	3.68
8.28	4.14	4.83	3	6.90	3.45	5.52
11.04	5.52	6.44	4	9.20	4.60	7.36
13.80	6.90	8.05	5	11.50	5.75	9.20
			MONTHS.			
23	12	13	1	19	10	15
46	23	27	2	38	19	31
69	35	40	3	58	29	46
92	46	54	4	77	38	61
1.15	58	67	5	96	48	77
1.38	69	81	**6**	1.15	58	92
1.61	81	94	7	1.34	67	1.07
1.84	92	1.07	8	1.53	77	1.23
2.07	1.04	1.21	9	1.73	86	1.38
2.30	1.15	1.34	10	1.92	96	1.53
2.53	1.27	1.48	11	2.11	1.05	1.69
			DAYS.			
01	0	0	1	01	0	01
02	01	01	2	01	01	01
02	01	01	3	02	01	02
03	02	02	4	03	01	02
04	02	02	**5**	03	02	03
05	02	03	6	04	02	03
05	03	03	7	04	02	04
06	03	04	8	05	03	04
07	03	04	9	06	03	05
08	04	04	**10**	06	03	05
08	04	05	11	07	04	06
09	05	05	12	08	04	06
10	05	06	13	08	04	07
11	05	06	14	09	04	07
12	06	07	**15**	10	05	08
12	06	07	16	10	05	08
13	07	08	17	11	05	09
14	07	08	18	12	06	09
15	07	08	19	12	06	10
15	08	09	**20**	13	06	10
16	08	09	21	13	07	11
17	08	10	22	14	07	11
18	09	10	23	15	07	12
18	09	11	24	15	08	12
19	10	11	**25**	16	08	13
20	10	12	26	17	08	13
21	10	12	27	17	09	14
21	11	13	28	18	09	14
22	11	13	29	19	09	15
23	12	13	**30**	19	10	15
25	13	15	33	21	11	17
48	24	28	63	40	20	32
71	36	42	93	59	30	47

24 Dollars.

12 PER CENT.	6 PER CENT.	7 PER CENT.	YEARS.	10 PER CENT.	5 PER CENT.	8 PER CENT.
2.88	1.44	1.68	1	2.40	1.20	1.92
5.76	2.88	3.36	2	4.80	2.40	3.84
8.64	4.32	5.04	3	7.20	3.60	5.76
11.52	5.76	6.72	4	9.60	4.80	7.68
14.40	7.20	8.40	5	12.00	6.00	9.60
			MONTHS.			
24	12	14	1	20	10	16
48	24	28	2	40	20	32
72	36	42	3	60	30	48
96	48	56	4	80	40	64
1.20	60	70	5	1.00	50	80
1.44	72	84	**6**	1.20	60	96
1.68	84	98	7	1.40	70	1.12
1.92	96	1.12	8	1.60	80	1.28
2.16	1.08	1.26	9	1.80	90	1.44
2.40	1.20	1.40	10	2.00	1.00	1.60
2.64	1.32	1.54	11	2.20	1.10	1.76
			DAYS.			
01	0	0	1	01	0	01
02	01	01	2	01	01	01
02	01	01	3	02	01	02
03	02	02	4	03	01	02
04	02	02	**5**	03	02	03
05	02	03	6	04	02	03
06	03	03	7	05	02	04
06	03	04	8	05	03	04
07	04	04	9	06	03	05
08	04	05	**10**	07	03	05
09	04	05	11	07	04	06
10	05	06	12	08	04	06
10	05	06	13	09	04	07
11	06	07	14	09	05	07
12	06	07	**15**	10	05	08
13	06	07	16	11	05	09
14	07	08	17	11	06	09
14	07	08	18	12	06	10
15	08	09	19	13	06	10
16	08	09	**20**	13	07	11
17	08	10	21	14	07	11
18	09	10	22	15	07	12
18	09	11	23	15	08	12
19	10	11	24	16	08	13
20	10	12	**25**	17	08	13
21	10	12	26	17	09	14
22	11	13	27	18	09	14
22	11	13	28	19	09	15
23	12	14	29	19	10	15
24	12	14	**30**	20	10	16
26	13	15	33	22	11	18
50	25	29	63	42	21	34
74	37	43	93	62	31	50

25 Dollars.

12 PER CENT.	6 PER CENT.	7 PER CENT.	YEARS.	10 PER CENT.	5 PER CENT.	8 PER CENT.
3.00	1.50	1.75	1	2.50	1.25	2.00
6.00	3.00	3.50	2	5.00	2.50	4.00
9.00	4.50	5.25	3	7.50	3.75	6.00
12.00	6.00	7.00	4	10.00	5.00	8.00
15.00	7.50	8.75	5	12.50	6.25	10.00
			MONTHS.			
25	13	15	1	21	10	17
50	25	29	2	42	21	33
75	38	44	3	63	31	50
1.00	50	58	4	83	42	67
1.25	63	73	5	1.04	52	83
1.50	75	88	**6**	1.25	63	1.00
1.75	88	1.02	7	1.46	73	1.17
2.00	1.00	1.17	8	1.67	83	1.33
2.25	1.13	1.31	9	1.88	94	1.50
2.50	1.25	1.46	10	2.08	1.04	1.67
2.75	1.38	1.60	11	2.29	1.15	1.83
			DAYS.			
01	0	0	1	01	0	01
02	01	01	2	01	01	01
03	01	01	3	02	01	02
03	02	02	4	03	01	02
04	02	02	**5**	03	02	03
05	03	03	6	04	02	03
06	03	03	7	05	02	04
07	03	04	8	06	03	04
08	04	04	9	06	03	05
08	04	05	**10**	07	03	06
09	05	05	11	08	04	06
10	05	06	12	08	04	07
11	05	06	13	09	05	07
12	06	07	14	10	05	08
13	06	07	**15**	10	05	08
13	07	08	16	11	06	09
14	07	08	17	12	06	09
15	08	09	18	13	06	10
16	08	09	19	13	07	11
17	08	10	**20**	14	07	11
18	09	10	21	15	07	12
18	09	11	22	15	08	12
19	10	11	23	16	08	13
20	10	12	24	17	08	13
21	10	12	**25**	17	09	14
22	11	13	26	18	09	14
23	11	13	27	19	09	15
23	12	14	28	19	10	16
24	12	14	29	20	10	16
25	13	15	**30**	21	10	17
27	14	16	33	23	11	19
52	26	31	63	44	22	36
77	39	45	93	64	32	53

26 Dollars.

12 PER CENT.	6 PER CENT.	7 PER CENT.	YEARS.	10 PER CENT.	5 PER CENT.	8 PER CENT.
3.12	1.56	1.82	1	2.60	1.30	2.08
6.24	3.12	3.64	2	5.20	2.60	4.16
9.36	4.68	5.46	3	7.80	3.90	6.24
12.48	6.24	7.28	4	10.40	5.20	8.32
15.60	7.80	9.10	5	13.00	6.50	10.40
			MONTHS.			
26	13	15	1	22	11	17
52	26	30	2	43	22	35
78	39	46	3	65	33	52
1.04	52	61	4	87	43	69
1.30	65	76	5	1.08	54	87
1.56	78	91	**6**	1.30	65	1.04
1.82	91	1.06	7	1.52	76	1.21
2.08	1.04	1.21	8	1.73	87	1.39
2.34	1.17	1.37	9	1.95	98	1.56
2.60	1.30	1.52	10	2.17	1.08	1.73
2.86	1.43	1.67	11	2.38	1.19	1.91
			DAYS.			
01	0	01	1	01	0	01
02	01	01	2	01	01	01
03	01	02	3	02	01	02
03	02	02	4	03	01	02
04	02	03	**5**	04	02	03
05	03	03	6	04	02	03
06	03	04	7	05	03	04
07	03	04	8	06	03	05
08	04	05	9	07	03	05
09	04	05	**10**	07	04	06
10	05	06	11	08	04	06
10	05	06	12	09	04	07
11	06	07	13	09	05	08
12	06	07	14	10	05	08
13	07	08	**15**	11	05	09
14	07	08	16	12	06	09
15	07	09	17	12	06	10
16	08	09	18	13	07	10
16	08	10	19	14	07	11
17	09	10	**20**	14	07	12
18	09	11	21	15	08	12
19	10	11	22	16	08	13
20	10	12	23	17	08	13
21	10	12	24	17	09	14
22	11	13	**25**	18	09	14
23	11	13	26	19	09	15
23	12	14	27	20	10	16
24	12	14	28	20	10	16
25	13	15	29	21	10	17
26	13	15	**30**	22	11	17
29	14	17	33	24	12	19
55	27	32	63	45	23	36
81	40	47	93	67	34	53

27 Dollars.

12 PER CENT.	6 PER CENT.	7 PER CENT.	YEARS.	10 PER CENT.	5 PER CENT.	8 PER CENT.
3.24	1.62	1.89	1	2.70	1.35	2.16
6.48	3.24	3.78	2	5.40	2.70	4.32
9.72	4.86	5.67	3	8.10	4.05	6.48
12.96	6.48	7.56	4	10.80	5.40	8.64
16.20	8.10	9.45	5	13.50	6.75	10.80
			MONTHS.			
27	14	16	1	23	11	18
54	27	32	2	45	23	36
81	41	47	3	68	34	54
1.08	54	63	4	90	45	72
1.35	68	79	5	1.13	56	90
1.62	81	95	**6**	1.35	68	1.08
1.89	95	1.10	7	1.58	79	1.26
2.16	1.08	1.26	8	1.80	90	1.44
2.43	1.22	1.42	9	2.03	1.01	1.62
2.70	1.35	1.58	10	2.25	1.13	1.80
2.97	1.49	1.73	11	2.48	1.24	1.98
			DAYS.			
01	0	01	1	01	0	01
02	01	01	2	01	01	01
03	01	02	3	02	01	02
04	02	02	4	03	02	02
05	02	03	**5**	04	02	03
05	03	03	6	05	02	04
06	03	04	7	05	03	04
07	04	04	8	06	03	05
08	04	05	9	07	03	05
09	05	05	**10**	08	04	06
10	05	06	11	08	04	07
11	05	06	12	09	05	07
12	06	07	13	10	05	08
13	03	07	14	11	05	08
14	07	08	**15**	11	06	09
14	0	08	16	12	06	10
15	08	09	17	13	06	10
16	08	09	18	14	07	11
17	09	10	19	14	07	11
18	09	11	**20**	15	08	12
19	09	11	21	16	08	13
20	10	12	22	17	08	13
21	10	12	23	17	09	14
22	11	13	24	18	09	14
23	11	13	**25**	19	09	15
23	12	14	26	20	10	16
24	12	14	27	20	10	16
25	13	15	28	21	11	17
26	13	15	29	22	11	17
27	14	16	**30**	23	11	18
30	15	17	33	25	12	20
57	28	34	63	48	23	38
84	42	50	93	70	35	56

28 Dollars.

12 PER CENT.	6 PER CENT.	7 PER CENT.	YEARS.	10 PER CENT.	5 PER CENT.	8 PER CENT.
3.36	1.68	1.96	1	2.80	1.40	2.24
6.72	3.36	3.92	2	5.60	2.80	4.48
10.08	5.04	5.88	3	8.40	4.20	6.72
13.44	6.72	7.84	4	11.20	5.60	8.96
16.80	8.40	9.80	5	14.00	7.00	11.20
			MONTHS.			
28	14	16	1	23	12	19
56	28	33	2	47	23	37
84	42	49	3	70	35	56
1.12	56	65	4	93	47	75
1.40	70	82	5	1.17	58	93
1.68	84	98	**6**	1.40	70	1.12
1.96	98	1.14	7	1.63	82	1.31
2.24	1.12	1.31	8	1.87	93	1.49
2.52	1.26	1.47	9	2.10	1.05	1.68
2.80	1.40	1.63	10	2.33	1.17	1.87
3.08	1.54	1.80	11	2.57	1.28	2.05
			DAYS.			
01	0	01	1	01	0	01
02	01	01	2	02	01	01
03	01	02	3	02	01	02
04	02	02	4	03	02	02
05	02	03	**5**	04	02	03
06	03	03	6	05	02	04
07	03	04	7	05	03	04
07	04	04	8	06	03	05
08	04	05	9	07	04	06
09	05	05	**10**	08	04	06
10	05	06	11	09	04	07
11	06	07	12	09	05	07
12	06	07	13	10	05	08
13	07	08	14	11	05	09
14	07	08	**15**	12	06	09
15	07	09	16	12	06	10
16	08	09	17	13	07	11
17	08	10	18	14	07	11
18	09	10	19	15	07	12
19	09	11	**20**	16	08	12
20	10	11	21	16	08	13
21	10	12	22	17	09	14
21	11	13	23	18	09	14
22	11	13	24	19	09	15
23	12	14	**25**	19	10	16
24	12	14	26	20	10	16
25	13	15	27	21	11	17
26	13	15	28	22	11	17
27	14	16	29	23	11	18
28	14	16	**30**	23	12	19
31	15	18	33	26	13	21
59	29	34	63	49	25	39
87	43	51	93	72	36	58

29 Dollars.

12 PER CENT.	6 PER CENT.	7 PER CENT.	YEARS.	10 PER CENT.	5 PER CENT.	8 PER CENT.
3.48	1.74	2.03	1	2.90	1.45	2.32
6.96	3.48	4.06	2	5.80	2.90	4.64
10.44	5.22	6.09	3	8.70	4.35	6.96
13.92	6.96	8.12	4	11.60	5.80	9.28
17.40	8.70	10.15	5	14.50	7.25	11.60
			MONTHS.			
29	15	17	1	24	12	19
58	29	34	2	48	24	39
87	44	51	3	73	36	58
1.16	58	68	4	97	48	77
1.45	73	85	5	1.21	60	97
1.74	87	1.02	**6**	1.45	73	1.16
2.03	1.02	1.18	7	1.69	85	1.35
2.32	1.16	1.35	8	1.93	97	1.55
2.61	1.31	1.52	9	2.18	1.09	1.74
2.90	1.45	1.69	10	2.42	1.21	1.93
3.19	1.60	1.86	11	2.66	1.33	2.13
			DAYS.			
01	0	01	1	01	0	01
02	01	01	2	02	01	01
03	01	02	3	02	01	02
04	02	02	4	03	02	03
05	02	03	**5**	04	02	03
06	03	03	6	05	02	04
07	03	04	7	06	03	05
08	04	05	8	06	03	05
09	04	05	9	07	04	06
10	05	06	**10**	08	04	06
11	05	06	11	09	04	07
12	06	07	12	10	05	08
13	06	07	13	10	05	08
14	07	08	14	11	06	09
15	07	08	**15**	12	06	10
15	08	09	16	13	06	10
16	08	10	17	14	07	11
17	09	10	18	15	07	12
18	09	11	19	15	08	12
19	10	11	**20**	16	08	13
20	10	12	21	17	08	14
21	11	12	22	18	09	14
22	11	13	23	19	09	15
23	12	14	24	19	10	15
24	12	14	**25**	20	10	16
25	13	15	26	21	10	17
26	13	15	27	22	11	17
27	14	16	28	23	11	18
28	14	16	29	23	12	19
29	15	17	**30**	24	12	19
32	16	19	33	26	13	21
61	30	36	63	51	25	41
90	45	52	93	75	37	60

30 Dollars.

12 PER CENT.	6 PER CENT.	7 PER CENT.	YEARS.	10 PER CENT.	5 PER CENT.	8 PER CENT.
3.60	1.80	2.10	1	3.00	1.50	2.40
7.20	3.60	4.20	2	6.00	3.00	4.80
10.80	5.40	6.30	3	9.00	4.50	7.20
14.40	7.20	8.40	4	12.00	6.00	9.60
18.00	9.00	10.50	5	15.00	7.50	12.00
			MONTHS.			
30	15	18	1	25	13	20
60	30	35	2	50	25	40
90	45	53	3	75	38	60
1.20	60	70	4	1.00	50	80
1.50	75	88	5	1.25	63	1.00
1.80	90	1.05	**6**	1.50	75	1.20
2.10	1.05	1.23	7	1.75	88	1.40
2.40	1.20	1.40	8	2.00	1.00	1.60
2.70	1.35	1.58	9	2.25	1.13	1.80
3.00	1.50	1.75	10	2.50	1.25	2.00
3.30	1.65	1.93	11	2.75	1.38	2.20
			DAYS.			
01	01	01	1	01	0	01
02	01	01	2	02	01	01
03	02	02	3	03	01	02
04	02	02	4	03	02	03
05	03	03	**5**	04	02	03
06	03	04	6	05	03	04
07	04	04	7	06	03	05
08	04	05	8	07	03	05
09	05	05	9	08	04	06
10	05	06	**10**	08	04	07
11	06	06	11	09	05	07
12	06	07	12	10	05	08
13	07	08	13	11	05	09
14	07	08	14	12	06	09
15	08	09	**15**	13	06	10
16	08	09	16	13	07	11
17	09	10	17	14	07	11
18	09	11	18	15	08	12
19	10	11	19	16	08	13
20	10	12	**20**	17	08	13
21	11	12	21	18	09	14
22	11	13	22	18	09	15
23	12	13	23	19	10	15
24	12	14	24	20	10	16
25	13	15	**25**	21	10	17
26	13	15	26	22	11	17
27	14	16	27	23	11	18
28	14	16	28	23	12	19
29	15	17	29	24	12	19
30	15	18	**30**	25	13	20
33	17	19	33	28	14	22
63	32	37	63	53	27	42
93	47	54	93	78	39	62

31 Dollars.

12 PER CENT.	6 PER CENT.	7 PER CENT.	YEARS.	10 PER CENT.	5 PER CENT.	8 PER CENT.
3.72	1.86	2.17	1	3.10	1.55	2.48
7.44	3.72	4.34	2	6.20	3.10	4.96
11.16	5.58	6.51	3	9.30	4.65	7.44
14.88	7.44	8.68	4	12.40	6.20	9.92
18.60	9.30	10.85	5	15.50	7.75	12.40
			MONTHS.			
31	16	18	1	26	13	21
62	31	36	2	52	26	41
93	47	54	3	78	39	62
1.24	62	72	4	1.03	52	83
1.55	78	90	5	1.29	65	1.03
1.86	93	1.09	**6**	1.55	78	1.24
2.17	1.09	1.27	7	1.81	90	1.45
2.48	1.24	1.45	8	2.07	1.03	1.65
2.79	1.40	1.63	9	2.33	1.16	1.86
3.10	1.55	1.81	10	2.58	1.29	2.07
3.41	1.71	1.99	11	2.84	1.42	2.27
			DAYS.			
01	01	01	1	01	0	01
02	01	01	2	02	01	01
03	02	02	3	03	01	02
04	02	02	4	03	02	03
05	03	03	**5**	04	02	03
06	03	04	6	05	03	04
07	04	04	7	06	03	05
08	04	05	8	07	03	06
09	05	05	9	08	04	06
10	05	06	**10**	09	04	07
11	06	07	11	09	05	08
12	06	07	12	10	05	08
13	07	08	13	11	06	09
14	07	08	14	12	06	10
16	08	09	**15**	13	06	10
17	08	10	16	14	07	11
18	09	10	17	15	07	12
19	09	11	18	16	08	12
20	10	11	19	16	08	13
21	10	12	**20**	17	09	14
22	11	13	21	18	09	14
23	11	13	22	19	09	15
24	12	14	23	20	10	16
25	12	14	24	21	10	17
26	13	15	**25**	22	11	17
27	13	16	26	22	11	18
28	14	16	27	23	12	19
29	14	17	28	24	12	19
30	15	17	29	25	12	20
31	16	18	**30**	26	13	21
34	19	20	33	28	14	23
65	33	38	63	54	27	44
96	48	56	93	80	40	64

32 Dollars.

12 PER CENT.	6 PER CENT.	7 PER CENT.	YEARS.	10 PER CENT.	5 PER CENT.	8 PER CENT.
3.84	1.92	2.24	1	3.20	1.60	2.56
7.68	3.84	4.48	2	6.40	3.20	5.12
11.52	5.76	6.72	3	9.60	4.80	7.68
15.36	7.68	8.96	4	12.80	6.40	10.24
19.20	9.60	11.20	5	16.00	8.00	12.80
			MONTHS.			
32	16	19	1	27	13	21
64	32	37	2	53	27	43
96	48	56	3	80	40	64
1.28	64	75	4	1.07	53	85
1.60	80	93	5	1.33	67	1.07
1.92	96	1.12	**6**	1.60	80	1.28
2.24	1.12	1.31	7	1.87	93	1.49
2.56	1.28	1.49	8	2.13	1.07	1.71
2.88	1.44	1.68	9	2.40	1.20	1.92
3.20	1.60	1.87	10	2.67	1.33	2.13
3.52	1.76	2.05	11	2.93	1.47	2.35
			DAYS.			
01	01	01	1	01	0	01
02	01	01	2	02	01	01
03	02	02	3	03	01	02
04	02	02	4	04	02	03
05	03	03	**5**	04	02	04
06	03	04	6	05	03	04
07	04	04	7	06	03	05
09	04	05	8	07	04	06
10	05	06	9	08	04	06
11	05	06	**10**	09	04	07
12	06	07	11	10	05	08
13	06	07	12	11	05	09
14	07	08	13	12	06	09
15	07	09	14	12	06	10
16	08	09	**15**	13	07	11
17	09	10	16	14	07	11
18	09	11	17	15	08	12
19	10	11	18	16	08	13
20	10	12	19	17	08	14
21	11	12	**20**	18	09	14
22	11	13	21	19	09	15
23	12	14	22	20	10	16
25	12	14	23	20	10	16
26	13	15	24	21	11	17
27	13	16	**25**	22	11	18
28	14	16	26	23	12	18
29	14	17	27	24	12	19
30	15	17	28	25	12	20
31	15	18	29	26	13	21
32	16	19	**30**	27	13	21
35	18	21	33	29	15	23
67	34	39	63	56	28	45
99	50	58	93	83	41	66

33 Dollars.

12 PER CENT.	6 PER CENT.	7 PER CENT.	YEARS.	10 PER CENT.	5 PER CENT.	8 PER CENT.
3.96	1.98	2.31	1	3.30	1.65	2.64
7.92	3.96	4.62	2	6.60	3.30	5.28
11.88	5.94	6.93	3	9.90	4.95	7.92
15.84	7.92	9.24	4	13.20	6.60	10.56
19.80	9.90	11.55	5	16.50	8.25	13.20
			MONTHS.			
33	17	19	1	28	14	22
66	33	39	2	55	28	44
99	50	58	3	83	41	66
1.32	66	77	4	1.10	55	88
1.65	83	96	5	1.38	69	1.10
1.98	99	1.16	**6**	1.65	83	1.32
2.31	1.16	1.35	7	1.93	96	1.54
2.64	1.32	1.54	8	2.20	1.10	1.76
2.97	1.49	1.73	9	2.48	1.24	1.98
3.30	1.65	1.93	10	2.75	1.38	2.20
3.63	1.82	2.12	11	3.03	1.51	2.42
			DAYS.			
01	01	01	1	01	0	01
02	01	01	2	02	01	01
03	02	02	3	03	01	02
04	02	03	4	04	02	03
06	03	03	**5**	05	02	04
07	03	04	6	06	03	04
08	04	04	7	06	03	05
09	04	05	8	07	04	06
10	05	06	9	08	04	07
11	06	06	**10**	09	05	07
12	06	07	11	10	05	08
13	07	08	12	11	06	09
14	07	08	13	12	06	10
15	08	09	14	13	06	10
17	08	10	**15**	14	07	11
18	09	10	16	15	07	12
19	09	11	17	16	08	12
20	10	12	18	17	08	13
21	10	12	19	17	09	14
22	11	13	**20**	18	09	15
23	12	13	21	19	10	15
24	12	14	22	20	10	16
25	13	15	23	21	11	17
26	13	15	24	22	11	18
28	14	16	**25**	23	11	18
29	14	17	26	24	12	19
30	15	17	27	25	12	20
31	15	18	28	26	13	21
32	16	19	29	27	13	21
33	17	19	**30**	28	14	22
36	18	21	33	30	15	24
69	35	40	63	58	29	46
1.02	51	60	93	85	43	68

34 Dollars.

12 PER CENT.	6 PER CENT.	7 PER CENT.	YEARS.	10 PER CENT.	5 PER CENT.	8 PER CENT.
4.08	2.04	2.38	1	3.40	1.70	2.72
8.16	4.08	4.76	2	6.80	3.40	5.44
12.24	6.12	7.14	3	10.20	5.10	8.16
16.32	8.16	9.52	4	13.60	6.80	10.88
20.40	10.20	11.90	5	17.00	8.50	13.60
			MONTHS.			
34	17	20	1	28	14	23
68	34	40	2	57	28	45
1.02	51	60	3	85	43	68
1.36	68	79	4	1.13	57	91
1.70	85	99	5	1.42	71	1.13
2.04	1.02	1.19	**6**	1.70	85	1.36
2.38	1.19	1.39	7	1.98	99	1.59
2.72	1.36	1.59	8	2.27	1.13	1.81
3.06	1.53	1.79	9	2.55	1.28	2.04
3.40	1.70	1.98	10	2.83	1.42	2.27
3.74	1.87	2.18	11	3.12	1.56	2.49
			DAYS.			
01	01	01	1	01	0	01
02	01	01	2	02	01	02
03	02	02	3	03	01	02
05	02	03	4	04	02	03
06	03	03	**5**	05	02	04
07	03	04	6	06	03	05
08	04	05	7	07	03	05
09	05	05	8	08	04	06
10	05	06	9	09	04	07
11	06	07	**10**	09	05	08
12	06	07	11	10	05	08
14	07	08	12	11	06	09
15	07	09	13	12	06	10
16	08	09	14	13	07	11
17	09	10	**15**	14	07	11
18	09	11	16	15	08	12
19	10	11	17	16	08	13
20	10	12	18	17	09	14
22	11	13	19	18	09	14
23	11	13	**20**	19	09	15
24	12	14	21	20	10	16
25	12	15	22	21	10	17
26	13	15	23	22	11	17
27	14	16	24	23	11	18
28	14	17	**25**	24	12	19
29	15	17	26	25	12	20
31	15	18	27	26	13	20
32	16	19	28	26	13	21
33	16	19	29	27	14	22
34	17	20	**30**	28	14	23
37	19	22	33	31	16	25
71	36	42	63	59	30	48
1.05	53	61	93	87	44	71

35 Dollars.

12 PER CENT.	6 PER CENT.	7 PER CENT.	YEARS.	10 PER CENT.	5 PER CENT.	8 PER CENT.
4.20	2.10	2.45	1	3.50	1.75	2.80
8.40	4.20	4.90	2	7.00	3.50	5.60
12.60	6.30	7.35	3	10.50	5.25	8.40
16.80	8.40	9.80	4	14.00	7.00	11.20
21.00	10.50	12.25	5	17.50	8.75	14.00
			MONTHS.			
35	18	20	1	29	15	23
70	35	41	2	58	29	47
1.05	53	61	3	88	44	70
1.40	70	82	4	1.17	58	93
1.75	88	1.02	5	1.46	73	1.17
2.10	1.05	1.23	**6**	1.75	88	1.40
2.45	1.23	1.43	7	2.04	1.02	1.63
2.80	1.40	1.63	8	2.33	1.17	1.87
3.15	1.58	1.84	9	2.63	1.31	2.10
3.50	1.75	2.04	10	2.92	1.46	2.33
3.85	1.93	2.25	11	3.21	1.60	2.57
			DAYS.			
01	01	01	1	01	0	01
02	01	01	2	02	01	02
04	02	02	3	03	01	02
05	02	03	4	04	02	03
06	03	03	**5**	05	02	04
07	04	04	6	06	03	05
08	04	05	7	07	03	05
09	05	05	8	08	04	06
11	05	06	9	09	04	07
12	06	07	**10**	10	05	08
13	06	07	11	11	05	09
14	07	08	12	12	06	09
15	08	09	13	13	06	10
16	08	10	14	14	07	11
18	09	10	**15**	15	07	12
19	09	11	16	16	08	12
20	10	12	17	17	08	13
21	11	12	18	18	09	14
22	11	13	19	18	09	15
23	12	14	**20**	19	10	16
25	12	14	21	20	10	16
26	13	15	22	21	11	17
27	13	16	23	22	11	18
28	14	16	24	23	12	19
29	15	17	**25**	24	12	19
30	15	18	26	25	13	20
32	16	18	27	26	13	21
33	16	19	28	27	14	22
34	17	20	29	28	14	23
35	18	20	**30**	29	15	23
39	19	22	33	32	16	26
74	37	43	63	61	31	49
1.09	54	63	93	90	45	72

36 Dollars.

12 PER CENT.	6 PER CENT.	7 PER CENT.	YEARS.	10 PER CENT.	5 PER CENT.	8 PER CENT.
4.32	2.16	2.52	1	3.60	1.80	2.88
8.64	4.32	5.04	2	7.20	3.60	5.76
12.96	6.48	7.56	3	10.80	5.40	8.64
17.28	8.64	10.08	4	14.40	7.20	11.52
21.60	10.80	12.60	5	18.00	9.00	14.40
			MONTHS.			
36	18	21	1	30	15	24
72	36	42	2	60	30	48
1.08	54	63	3	90	45	72
1.44	72	84	4	1.20	60	96
1.80	90	1.05	5	1.50	75	1.20
2.16	1.08	1.26	**6**	1.80	90	1.44
2.52	1.26	1.47	7	2.10	1.05	1.68
2.88	1.44	1.68	8	2.40	1.20	1.92
3.24	1.62	1.89	9	2.70	1.35	2.16
3.60	1.80	2.10	10	3.00	1.50	2.40
3.96	1.98	2.31	11	3.30	1.65	2.64
			DAYS.			
01	01	01	1	01	01	01
02	01	01	2	02	01	02
04	02	02	3	03	02	02
05	02	03	4	04	02	03
06	03	04	**5**	05	03	04
07	04	04	6	06	03	05
08	04	05	7	07	04	06
10	05	06	8	08	04	06
11	05	06	9	09	05	07
12	06	07	**10**	10	05	08
13	07	08	11	11	06	09
14	07	08	12	12	06	10
16	08	09	13	13	07	10
17	08	10	14	14	07	11
18	09	11	**15**	15	08	12
19	10	11	16	16	08	13
20	10	12	17	17	09	14
22	11	13	18	18	09	14
23	11	13	19	19	10	15
24	12	14	**20**	20	10	16
25	13	15	21	21	11	17
26	13	15	22	22	11	18
28	14	16	23	23	12	18
29	14	17	24	24	12	19
30	15	18	**25**	25	13	20
31	16	18	26	26	13	21
32	16	19	27	27	14	22
34	17	20	28	28	14	22
35	17	20	29	29	15	23
36	18	21	**30**	30	15	24
40	20	23	33	33	17	26
76	38	44	63	63	32	50
1.12	56	65	93	93	47	74

37 Dollars.

12 PER CENT.	6 PER CENT.	7 PER CENT.	YEARS.	10 PER CENT.	5 PER CENT.	8 PER CENT.
4.44	2.22	2.59	1	3.70	1.85	2.96
8.88	4.44	5.18	2	7.40	3.70	5.92
13.32	6.66	7.77	3	11.10	5.55	8.88
17.76	8.88	10.36	4	14.80	7.40	11.84
22.20	11.10	12.95	5	18.50	9.25	14.80
			MONTHS.			
37	19	22	1	31	15	25
74	37	43	2	62	31	49
1.11	56	65	3	93	46	74
1.48	74	86	4	1.23	62	99
1.85	93	1.08	5	1.54	77	1.23
2.22	1.11	1.30	**6**	1.85	93	1.48
2.59	1.30	1.51	7	2.16	1.08	1.73
2.96	1.48	1.73	8	2.47	1.23	1.97
3.33	1.67	1.94	9	2.78	1.39	2.22
3.70	1.85	2.16	10	3.08	1.54	2.47
4.07	2.04	2.37	11	3.39	1.70	2.71
			DAYS.			
01	01	01	1	01	01	01
02	01	01	2	02	01	02
04	02	02	3	03	02	02
05	02	03	4	04	02	03
06	03	04	**5**	05	03	04
07	04	04	6	06	03	05
09	04	05	7	07	04	06
10	05	06	8	08	04	07
11	06	06	9	09	05	07
12	06	07	**10**	10	05	08
14	07	08	11	11	06	09
15	07	09	12	12	06	10
16	08	09	13	13	07	11
17	09	10	14	14	07	12
19	09	11	**15**	15	08	12
20	10	12	16	16	08	13
21	10	12	17	17	09	14
22	11	13	18	19	09	15
23	12	14	19	20	10	16
25	12	14	**20**	21	10	16
26	13	15	21	22	11	17
27	14	16	22	23	11	18
28	14	17	23	24	12	19
30	15	17	24	25	12	20
31	15	18	**25**	26	13	21
32	16	19	26	27	13	21
33	17	19	27	28	14	22
35	17	20	28	29	14	23
36	18	21	29	30	15	24
37	19	22	**30**	31	15	25
41	20	24	33	34	17	27
78	39	45	63	65	32	52
1.15	57	67	93	96	48	77

38 Dollars.

12 PER CENT.	6 PER CENT.	7 PER CENT.	YEARS.	10 PER CENT.	5 PER CENT.	8 PER CENT.
4.56	2.28	2.66	1	3.80	1.90	3.04
9.12	4.56	5.32	2	7.60	3.80	6.08
13.68	6.84	7.98	3	11.40	5.70	9.12
18.24	9.12	10.64	4	15.20	7.60	12.16
22.80	11.40	13.30	5	19.00	9.50	15.20
			MONTHS.			
38	19	22	1	32	16	25
76	38	44	2	63	32	51
1.14	57	67	3	95	48	76
1.52	76	89	4	1.27	63	1.01
1.90	95	1.11	5	1.58	79	1.27
2.28	1.14	1.33	**6**	1.90	95	1.52
2.66	1.33	1.55	7	2.22	1.11	1.77
3.04	1.52	1.77	8	2.53	1.27	2.03
3.42	1.71	2.00	9	2.85	1.43	2.28
3.80	1.90	2.22	10	3.17	1.58	2.53
4.18	2.09	2.44	11	3.48	1.74	2.79
			DAYS.			
01	01	01	1	01	01	01
03	01	01	2	02	01	02
04	02	02	3	03	02	03
05	03	03	4	04	02	03
06	03	04	**5**	05	03	04
08	04	04	6	06	03	05
09	04	05	7	07	04	06
10	05	06	8	08	04	07
11	06	07	9	10	05	08
13	06	07	**10**	11	05	08
14	07	08	11	12	06	09
15	08	09	12	13	06	10
16	08	10	13	14	07	11
18	09	10	14	15	07	12
19	10	11	**15**	16	08	13
20	10	12	16	17	08	14
22	11	13	17	18	09	14
23	11	13	18	19	10	15
24	12	14	19	20	10	16
25	13	15	**20**	21	11	17
27	13	16	21	22	11	18
28	14	16	22	23	12	19
29	15	17	23	24	12	19
30	15	18	24	25	13	20
32	16	18	**25**	26	13	21
33	16	19	26	27	14	22
34	17	20	27	29	14	23
35	18	21	28	30	15	24
37	18	21	29	31	15	24
38	19	22	**30**	32	16	25
41	21	24	33	35	17	28
80	40	47	63	67	33	53
1.18	59	69	93	98	49	78

39 Dollars.

12 PER CENT.	6 PER CENT.	7 PER CENT.	YEARS.	10 PER CENT.	5 PER CENT.	8 PER CENT.
4.68	2.34	2.73	1	3.90	1.95	3.12
9.36	4.68	5.46	2	7.80	3.90	6.24
14.04	7.02	8.19	3	11.70	5.85	9.36
18.72	9.36	10.92	4	15.60	7.80	12.48
23.40	11.70	13.65	5	19.50	9.75	15.60
			MONTHS.			
39	20	23	1	33	16	26
78	39	46	2	65	33	52
1.17	59	68	3	98	49	78
1.56	78	91	4	1.30	65	1.04
1.95	98	1.14	5	1.63	81	1.30
2.34	1.17	1.37	**6**	1.95	98	1.56
2.73	1.37	1.59	7	2.28	1.14	1.82
3.12	1.56	1.82	8	2.60	1.30	2.08
3.51	1.76	2.05	9	2.93	1.46	2.34
3.90	1.95	2.28	10	3.25	1.63	2.60
4.29	2.15	2.50	11	3.58	1.79	2.86
			DAYS.			
01	01	01	1	01	01	01
03	01	02	2	02	01	02
04	02	02	3	03	02	03
05	03	03	4	04	02	03
07	03	04	**5**	05	03	04
08	04	05	6	07	03	05
09	05	05	7	08	04	06
10	05	06	8	09	04	07
12	06	07	9	10	05	08
13	07	08	**10**	11	05	09
14	07	08	11	12	06	10
16	08	09	12	13	07	10
17	08	10	13	14	07	11
18	09	11	14	15	08	12
20	10	11	**15**	16	08	13
21	10	12	16	17	09	14
22	11	13	17	18	09	15
23	12	14	18	20	10	16
25	12	14	19	21	10	16
26	13	15	**20**	22	11	17
27	14	16	**21**	23	11	18
29	14	17	**22**	24	12	19
30	15	17	**23**	25	12	20
31	16	18	24	26	13	21
33	16	19	**25**	27	14	22
34	17	20	26	28	14	23
35	18	20	27	29	15	23
36	18	21	28	30	15	24
38	19	22	29	31	16	25
39	20	23	**30**	33	16	26
43	21	25	33	36	18	29
82	41	48	63	68	34	55
1.21	60	71	93	1.01	50	81

40 Dollars.

12 PER CENT.	6 PER CENT.	7 PER CENT.	YEARS.	10 PER CENT.	5 PER CENT.	8 PER CENT.
4.80	2.40	2.80	1	4.00	2.00	3.20
9.60	4.80	5.60	2	8.00	4.00	6.40
14.40	7.20	8.40	3	12.00	6.00	9.60
19.20	9.60	11.20	4	16.00	8.00	12.80
24.00	12.00	14.00	5	20.00	10.00	16.00
			MONTHS.			
40	20	23	1	33	17	27
80	40	47	2	67	33	53
1.20	60	70	3	1.00	50	80
1.60	80	93	4	1.33	67	1.07
2.00	1.00	1.17	5	1.67	83	1.33
2.40	1.20	1.40	**6**	2.00	1.00	1.60
2.80	1.40	1.63	7	2.33	1.17	1.87
3.20	1.60	1.87	8	2.67	1.33	2.13
3.60	1.80	2.10	9	3.00	1.50	2.40
4.00	2.00	2.33	10	3.33	1.67	2.67
4.40	2.20	2.57	11	3.67	1.83	2.93
			DAYS.			
01	01	01	1	01	01	01
03	01	02	2	02	01	02
04	02	02	3	03	02	03
05	03	03	4	04	02	04
07	03	04	**5**	06	03	04
08	04	05	6	07	03	05
09	05	05	7	08	04	06
11	05	06	8	09	04	07
12	06	07	9	10	05	08
13	07	08	**10**	11	06	09
15	07	09	11	12	06	10
16	08	09	12	13	07	11
17	09	10	13	14	07	12
19	09	11	14	16	08	12
20	10	12	**15**	17	08	13
21	11	12	16	18	09	14
23	11	13	17	19	09	15
24	12	14	18	20	10	16
25	13	15	19	21	11	17
27	13	16	**20**	22	11	18
28	14	16	21	23	12	19
29	15	17	22	24	12	20
31	15	18	23	26	13	20
32	16	19	24	27	13	21
33	17	19	**25**	28	14	22
35	17	20	26	29	14	23
36	18	21	27	30	15	24
37	19	22	28	31	16	25
39	19	23	29	32	16	26
40	20	23	**30**	33	17	27
44	22	25	33	37	18	29
84	42	48	63	70	35	56
1.24	62	71	93	1.03	52	83

41 Dollars.

12 PER CENT.	6 PER CENT.	7 PER CENT.	YEARS.	10 PER CENT.	5 PER CENT.	8 PER CENT.
4.92	2.46	2.87	1	4.10	2.05	3.28
9.84	4.92	5.74	2	8.20	4.10	6.56
14.76	7.38	8.61	3	12.30	6.15	9.84
19.68	9.84	11.48	4	16.40	8.20	13.12
24.60	12.30	14.35	5	20.50	10.25	16.40
			MONTHS.			
41	21	24	1	34	17	27
82	41	48	2	68	34	55
1.23	62	72	3	1.03	51	82
1.64	82	96	4	1.37	68	1.09
2.05	1.03	1.20	5	1.71	85	1.37
2.46	1.23	1.44	**6**	2.05	1.03	1.64
2.87	1.44	1.67	7	2.39	1.20	1.91
3.28	1.64	1.91	8	2.73	1.37	2.19
3.69	1.85	2.15	9	3.08	1.54	2.46
4.10	2.05	2.39	10	3.42	1.71	2.73
4.51	2.26	2.63	11	3.76	1.88	3.01
			DAYS.			
01	01	01	1	01	01	01
03	01	02	2	02	01	02
04	02	02	3	03	02	03
05	03	03	4	05	02	04
07	03	04	**5**	06	03	05
08	04	05	6	07	03	05
10	05	06	7	08	04	06
11	05	06	8	09	05	07
12	06	07	9	10	05	08
14	07	08	**10**	11	06	09
15	08	09	11	13	06	10
16	08	10	12	14	07	11
18	09	10	13	15	07	12
19	10	11	14	16	08	13
21	10	12	**15**	17	09	14
22	11	13	16	18	09	15
23	12	14	17	19	10	15
25	12	14	18	21	10	16
26	13	15	19	22	11	17
27	14	16	**20**	23	11	18
29	14	17	21	24	12	19
30	15	18	22	25	13	20
31	16	18	23	26	13	21
33	16	19	24	27	14	22
34	17	20	**25**	28	14	23
36	18	21	26	30	15	24
37	18	22	27	31	15	25
38	19	22	28	32	16	26
40	20	23	29	33	17	26
41	21	24	**30**	34	17	27
45	23	26	33	38	19	30
86	43	50	63	72	36	57
1.27	64	74	93	1.06	53	84

42 Dollars.

12 PER CENT.	6 PER CENT.	7 PER CENT.	YEARS.	10 PER CENT.	5 PER CENT.	8 PER CENT.
5.04	2.52	2.94	1	4.20	2.10	3.36
10.08	5.04	5.88	2	8.40	4.20	6.72
15.12	7.56	8.82	3	12.60	6.30	10.08
20.16	10.08	11.76	4	16.80	8.40	13.44
25.20	12.60	14.70	5	21.00	10.50	16.80
			MONTHS.			
42	21	25	1	35	18	28
84	42	49	2	70	35	56
1.26	63	74	3	1.05	53	84
1.68	84	98	4	1.40	70	1.12
2.10	1.05	1.23	5	1.75	88	1.40
2.52	1.26	1.47	**6**	2.10	1.05	1.68
2.94	1.47	1.72	7	2.45	1.23	1.96
3.36	1.68	1.96	8	2.80	1.40	2.24
3.78	1.89	2.21	9	3.15	1.58	2.52
4.20	2.10	2.45	10	3.50	1.75	2.80
4.62	2.31	2.70	11	3.85	1.93	3.08
			DAYS.			
01	01	01	1	01	01	01
03	01	02	2	02	01	02
04	02	02	3	04	02	03
06	03	03	4	05	02	04
07	04	04	**5**	06	03	05
08	04	05	6	07	04	06
10	05	06	7	08	04	07
11	06	07	8	09	05	07
13	06	07	9	11	05	08
14	07	08	**10**	12	06	09
15	08	09	11	13	06	10
17	08	10	12	14	07	11
18	09	11	13	15	08	12
20	10	11	14	16	08	13
21	11	12	**15**	18	09	14
22	11	13	16	19	09	15
24	12	14	17	20	10	16
25	13	15	18	21	11	17
27	13	16	19	22	11	18
28	14	16	**20**	23	12	19
29	15	17	21	24	12	20
31	15	18	22	26	13	21
32	16	19	23	27	13	21
34	17	20	24	28	14	22
35	18	20	**25**	29	15	23
36	18	21	26	30	15	24
38	19	22	27	32	16	25
39	20	23	28	33	16	26
41	20	24	29	34	17	27
42	21	25	**30**	35	18	28
46	23	27	33	38	19	31
88	44	51	63	73	37	59
1.30	65	76	93	1.08	54	87

43 Dollars.

12 PER CENT.	6 PER CENT.	7 PER CENT.	YEARS.	10 PER CENT.	5 PER CENT.	8 PER CENT.
5.16	2.58	3.01	1	4.30	2.15	3.44
10.32	5.16	6.02	2	8.60	4.30	6.88
15.48	7.74	9.03	3	12.90	6.45	10.32
20.64	10.32	12.04	4	17.20	8.60	13.76
25.80	12.90	15.05	5	21.50	10.75	17.20
			MONTHS.			
43	22	25	1	36	18	29
86	43	50	2	72	36	57
1.29	65	75	3	1.08	54	86
1.72	86	1.00	4	1.43	72	1.15
2.15	1.08	1.25	5	1.79	90	1.43
2.58	1.29	1.51	**6**	2.15	1.08	1.72
3.01	1.51	1.76	7	2.51	1.25	2.01
3.44	1.72	2.01	8	2.87	1.43	2.29
3.87	1.94	2.26	9	3.23	1.61	2.58
4.30	2.15	2.51	10	3.58	1.79	2.87
4.73	2.37	2.76	11	3.94	1.97	3.15
			DAYS.			
01	01	01	1	01	01	01
03	01	02	2	02	01	02
04	02	03	3	04	02	03
06	03	03	4	05	02	04
07	04	04	**5**	06	03	05
09	04	05	6	07	04	06
10	05	06	7	08	04	07
11	06	07	8	10	05	08
13	06	08	9	11	05	09
14	07	08	**10**	12	06	10
16	08	09	11	13	07	11
17	09	10	12	14	07	11
19	09	11	13	16	08	12
20	10	12	14	17	08	13
22	11	13	**15**	18	09	14
23	11	13	16	19	10	15
24	12	14	17	20	10	16
26	13	15	18	22	11	17
27	14	16	19	23	11	18
29	14	17	**20**	24	12	19
30	15	18	21	25	13	20
32	16	18	22	26	13	21
33	16	19	23	27	14	22
34	17	20	24	29	14	23
36	18	21	**25**	30	15	24
37	19	22	26	31	16	25
39	19	23	27	32	16	26
40	20	23	28	33	17	27
42	21	24	29	35	17	28
43	22	25	**30**	36	18	29
47	24	28	33	39	20	32
90	45	53	63	75	38	60
1.33	67	78	93	1.11	55	89

44 Dollars.

12 PER CENT.	6 PER CENT.	7 PER CENT.	YEARS.	10 PER CENT.	5 PER CENT.	8 PER CENT.
5.28	2.64	3.08	1	4.40	2.20	3.52
10.56	5.28	6.16	2	8.80	4.40	7.04
15.84	7.92	9.24	3	13.20	6.60	10.56
21.12	10.56	12.32	4	17.60	8.80	14.08
26.40	13.20	15.40	5	22.00	11.00	17.60
			MONTHS.			
44	22	26	1	37	18	29
88	44	51	2	73	37	59
1.32	66	77	3	1.10	55	88
1.76	88	1.03	4	1.47	73	1.17
2.20	1.10	1.28	5	1.83	92	1.47
2.64	1.32	1.54	**6**	2.20	1.10	1.76
3.08	1.54	1.80	7	2.57	1.28	2.05
3.52	1.76	2.05	8	2.93	1.47	2.35
3.96	1.98	2.31	9	3.30	1.65	2.64
4.40	2.20	2.57	10	3.67	1.83	2.93
4.84	2.42	2.82	11	4.03	2.02	3.23
			DAYS.			
01	01	01	1	01	01	01
03	01	02	2	02	01	02
04	02	03	3	04	02	03
06	03	03	4	05	02	04
07	04	04	**5**	06	03	05
09	04	05	6	07	04	06
10	05	06	7	09	04	07
12	06	07	8	10	05	08
13	07	08	9	11	06	09
15	07	09	**10**	12	06	10
16	08	09	11	13	07	11
18	09	10	12	15	07	12
19	10	11	13	16	08	13
21	10	12	14	17	09	14
22	11	13	**15**	18	09	15
23	12	14	16	20	10	16
25	12	15	17	21	10	17
26	13	15	18	22	11	18
28	14	16	19	23	12	19
29	15	17	**20**	24	12	20
31	15	18	21	26	13	21
32	16	19	22	27	13	22
34	17	20	23	28	14	22
35	18	21	24	29	15	23
37	18	21	**25**	31	15	24
38	19	22	26	32	16	25
40	20	23	27	33	17	26
41	21	24	28	34	17	27
43	21	25	29	35	18	28
44	22	26	**30**	37	18	29
48	24	28	33	40	20	32
92	46	54	63	77	38	62
1.36	68	80	93	1.13	57	91

45 Dollars.

12 PER CENT.	6 PER CENT.	7 PER CENT.	YEARS.	10 PER CENT.	5 PER CENT.	8 PER CENT.
5.40	2.70	3.15	1	4.50	2.25	3.60
10.80	5.40	6.30	2	9.00	4.50	7.20
16.20	8.10	9.45	3	13.50	6.75	10.80
21.60	10.80	12.60	4	18.00	9.00	14.40
27.00	13.50	15.75	5	22.50	11.25	18.00
			MONTHS.			
45	23	26	1	38	19	30
90	45	53	2	75	38	60
1.35	68	79	3	1.13	56	90
1.80	90	1.05	4	1.50	75	1.20
2.25	1.13	1.31	5	1.88	94	1.50
2.70	1.35	1.58	**6**	2.25	1.13	1.80
3.15	1.58	1.84	7	2.62	1.31	2.10
3.60	1.80	2.10	8	3.00	1.50	2.40
4.05	2.03	2.36	9	3.38	1.69	2.70
4.50	2.25	2.63	10	3.75	1.88	3.00
4.95	2.48	2.89	11	4.13	2.06	3.30
			DAYS.			
02	01	01	1	01	01	01
03	02	02	2	03	01	02
05	02	03	3	04	02	03
06	03	04	4	05	03	04
08	04	04	**5**	06	03	05
09	05	05	6	08	04	06
11	05	06	7	09	04	07
12	06	07	8	10	05	08
14	07	08	9	11	06	09
15	08	09	**10**	13	06	10
17	08	10	11	14	07	11
18	09	11	12	15	08	12
20	10	11	13	16	08	13
21	11	12	14	18	09	14
23	11	13	**15**	19	09	15
24	12	14	16	20	10	16
26	13	15	17	21	11	17
27	14	16	18	23	11	18
29	14	17	19	24	12	19
30	15	18	**20**	25	13	20
32	16	18	21	26	13	21
33	17	19	22	28	14	22
35	17	20	23	29	14	23
36	18	21	24	30	15	24
38	19	22	**25**	31	16	25
39	20	23	26	33	16	26
41	20	24	27	34	17	27
42	21	25	28	35	18	28
44	22	25	29	36	18	29
45	23	26	**30**	38	19	30
50	25	29	33	41	21	33
95	47	55	63	79	39	63
1.40	70	81	93	1.16	58	93

46 Dollars.

12 PER CENT.	6 PER CENT.	7 PER CENT.	YEARS.	10 PER CENT.	5 PER CENT.	8 PER CENT.
5.52	2.76	3.22	1	4.60	2.30	3.68
11.04	5.52	6.44	2	9.20	4.60	7.36
16.56	8.28	9.66	3	13.80	6.90	11.04
22.08	11.04	12.88	4	18.40	9.20	14.72
27.60	13.80	16.10	5	23.00	11.50	18.40
			MONTHS.			
46	23	27	1	38	19	31
92	46	54	2	77	38	61
1.38	69	81	3	1.15	58	92
1.84	92	1.07	4	1.53	77	1.23
2.30	1.15	1.34	5	1.92	96	1.53
2.76	1.38	1.61	**6**	2.30	1.15	1.84
3·22	1.61	1.88	7	2.68	1.34	2.15
3.68	1.84	2.15	8	3.07	1.53	2.45
4.14	2.07	2.42	9	3.45	1.73	2.76
4.60	2.30	2.68	**10**	3.83	1.92	3.07
5.06	2.53	2.95	**11**	4.22	2.11	3.37
			DAYS.			
02	01	01	1	01	01	01
03	02	02	2	03	01	02
05	02	03	3	04	02	03
06	03	04	4	05	03	04
08	04	04	**5**	06	03	05
09	05	05	6	08	04	06
11	05	06	7	09	04	07
12	06	07	8	10	05	08
14	07	08	9	12	06	09
15	08	09	**10**	13	06	10
17	08	10	11	14	07	11
18	09	11	12	15	08	12
20	10	12	13	17	08	13
21	11	13	14	18	09	14
23	12	13	**15**	19	10	15
25	12	14	16	20	10	16
26	13	15	17	22	11	17
28	14	16	18	23	12	18
29	15	17	19	24	12	19
31	15	18	**20**	26	13	20
32	16	19	21	27	13	21
34	17	20	22	28	14	22
35	18	21	23	29	15	24
37	18	21	24	31	15	25
38	19	22	**25**	32	16	26
40	20	23	26	33	17	27
41	21	24	27	35	17	28
43	21	25	28	36	18	29
44	22	26	29	37	19	30
46	23	27	**30**	38	19	31
51	25	30	33	42	21	34
97	48	56	63	80	40	65
1.43	71	83	93	1.18	59	96

47 Dollars.

12 PER CENT.	6 PER CENT.	7 PER CENT.	YEARS.	10 PER CENT.	5 PER CENT.	8 PER CENT.
5.64	2.82	3.29	1	4.70	2.35	3.76
11.28	5.64	6.58	2	9.40	4.70	7.52
16.92	8.46	9.87	3	14.10	7.05	11.28
22.56	11.28	13.16	4	18.80	9.40	15.04
28.20	14.10	16.45	5	23.50	11.75	18.80
			MONTHS.			
47	24	27	1	39	20	31
94	47	55	2	78	39	63
1.41	71	82	3	1.18	59	94
1.88	94	1.10	4	1.57	78	1.25
2.35	1.18	1.37	5	1.96	98	1.57
2.82	1.41	1.65	**6**	2.35	1.18	1.88
3.29	1.65	1.92	7	2.74	1.37	2.19
3.76	1.88	2.19	8	3.13	1.57	2.51
4.23	2.12	2.47	9	3.53	1.76	2.82
4.70	2.35	2.74	10	3.92	1.96	3.13
5.17	2.59	3.02	11	4.31	2.15	3.45
			DAYS.			
02	01	01	1	01	01	01
03	02	02	2	03	01	02
05	02	03	3	04	02	03
06	03	04	4	05	03	04
08	04	05	**5**	07	03	05
09	05	05	6	08	04	06
11	05	06	7	09	05	07
13	06	07	8	10	05	08
14	07	08	9	12	06	09
16	08	09	**10**	13	07	10
17	09	10	11	14	07	11
19	09	11	12	16	08	13
20	10	12	13	17	08	14
22	11	13	14	18	09	15
24	12	14	**15**	20	10	16
25	13	15	16	21	10	17
27	13	16	17	22	11	18
28	14	16	18	24	12	19
30	15	17	19	25	12	20
31	16	18	**20**	26	13	21
33	16	19	21	27	14	22
34	17	20	22	29	14	23
36	18	21	23	30	15	24
38	19	22	24	31	16	25
39	20	23	**25**	33	16	26
41	20	24	26	34	17	27
42	21	25	27	35	18	28
44	22	26	28	37	18	29
45	23	27	29	38	19	30
47	24	27	**30**	39	20	31
51	25	30	33	43	22	34
98	49	58	63	82	41	66
1.45	73	85	93	1.21	61	97

48 Dollars.

12 PER CENT.	6 PER CENT.	7 PER CENT.	YEARS.	10 PER CENT.	5 PER CENT.	8 PER CENT.
5.76	2.88	3.36	1	4.80	2.40	3.84
11.52	5.76	6.72	2	9.60	4.80	7.68
17.28	8.64	10.08	3	14.40	7.20	11.52
23.04	11.52	13.44	4	19.20	9.60	15.36
28.80	14.40	16.80	5	24.00	12.00	19.20
			MONTHS.			
48	24	28	1	40	20	32
96	48	56	2	80	40	64
1.44	72	84	3	1.20	60	96
1.92	96	1.12	4	1.60	80	1.28
2.40	1.20	1.40	5	2.00	1.00	1.60
2.88	1.44	1.68	**6**	2.40	1.20	1.92
3.36	1.68	1.96	7	2.80	1.40	2.24
3.84	1.92	2.24	8	3.20	1.60	2.56
4.32	2.16	2.52	9	3.60	1.80	2.88
4.80	2.40	2.80	10	4.00	2.00	3.20
5.28	2.64	3.08	11	4.40	2.20	3.52
			DAYS.			
02	01	01	1	01	01	01
03	02	02	2	03	01	02
05	02	03	3	04	02	03
06	03	04	4	05	03	04
08	04	05	**5**	07	03	05
10	05	06	6	08	04	06
11	06	07	7	09	05	07
13	06	07	8	11	05	09
14	07	08	9	12	06	10
16	08	09	**10**	13	07	11
18	09	10	11	15	07	12
19	10	11	12	16	08	13
21	10	12	13	17	09	14
22	11	13	14	19	09	15
24	12	14	**15**	20	10	16
26	13	15	16	21	11	17
27	14	16	17	23	11	18
29	14	17	18	24	12	19
30	15	18	19	25	13	20
32	16	19	**20**	27	13	21
34	17	20	21	28	14	22
35	18	21	22	29	15	23
37	18	21	23	31	15	25
38	19	22	24	32	16	26
40	20	23	**25**	33	17	27
42	21	24	26	35	17	28
43	22	25	27	36	18	29
45	22	26	28	37	19	30
46	23	27	29	39	19	31
48	24	28	**30**	40	20	32
53	26	31	33	44	22	35
1.01	50	59	63	84	42	67
1.49	74	87	93	1.24	62	99

49 Dollars.

12 PER CENT.	6 PER CENT.	7 PER CENT.	YEARS.	10 PER CENT.	5 PER CENT.	8 PER CENT.
5.88	2.94	3.43	1	4.90	2.45	3.92
11.76	5.88	6.86	2	9.80	4.90	7.84
17.64	8.82	10.29	3	14.70	7.35	11.76
23.52	11.76	13.72	4	19.60	9.80	15.68
29.40	14.70	17.15	5	24.50	12.25	19.60
			MONTHS.			
49	25	29	1	41	20	33
98	49	57	2	82	41	65
1.47	74	86	3	1.23	61	98
1.96	98	1.14	4	1.63	82	1.31
2.45	1.23	1.43	5	2.04	1.02	1.63
2.94	1.47	1.72	**6**	2.45	1.23	1.96
3.43	1.72	2.00	7	2.86	1.43	2.29
3.92	1.96	2.29	8	3.27	1.63	2.61
4.41	2.21	2.57	9	3.68	1.84	2.94
4.90	2.45	2.86	10	4.08	2.04	3.27
5.39	2.70	3.14	11	4.49	2.25	3.59
			DAYS.			
02	01	01	1	01	01	01
03	02	02	2	03	01	02
05	02	03	3	04	02	03
07	03	04	4	05	03	04
08	04	05	**5**	07	03	05
10	05	06	6	08	04	07
11	06	07	7	10	05	08
13	07	08	8	11	05	09
15	07	09	9	12	06	10
16	08	10	**10**	14	07	11
18	09	10	11	15	07	12
20	10	11	12	16	08	13
21	11	12	13	18	09	14
23	11	13	14	19	10	15
25	12	14	**15**	20	10	16
26	13	15	16	22	11	17
28	14	16	17	23	12	19
29	15	17	18	25	12	20
31	16	18	19	26	13	21
33	16	19	**20**	27	14	22
34	17	20	21	29	14	23
36	18	21	22	30	15	24
38	19	22	23	31	16	25
39	20	23	24	33	16	26
41	20	24	**25**	34	17	27
42	21	25	26	35	18	28
44	22	26	27	37	18	29
46	23	27	28	38	19	30
47	24	28	29	39	20	32
49	25	29	**30**	41	20	33
54	27	31	33	45	22	36
1.03	51	60	63	85	43	69
1.52	76	89	93	1.26	63	1.01

50 Dollars.

12 PER CENT.	6 PER CENT.	7 PER CENT.	YEARS.	10 PER CENT.	5 PER CENT.	8 PER CENT.
6.00	3.00	3.50	1	5.00	2.50	4.00
12.00	6.00	7.00	2	10.00	5.00	8.00
18.00	9.00	10.50	3	15.00	7.50	12.00
24.00	12.00	14.00	4	20.00	10.00	16.00
30.00	15.00	17.50	5	25.00	12.50	20.00
			MONTHS.			
50	25	29	1	42	21	33
1.00	50	58	2	83	42	67
1.50	75	88	3	1.25	63	1.00
2.00	1.00	1.17	4	1.67	83	1.33
2.50	1.25	1.46	5	2.08	1.04	1.67
3.00	1.50	1.75	**6**	2.50	1.25	2.00
3.50	1.75	2.04	7	2.92	1.46	2.33
4.00	2.00	2.33	8	3.33	1.67	2.67
4.50	2.25	2.63	9	3.75	1.88	3.00
5.00	2.50	2.92	10	4.17	2.08	3.33
5.50	2.75	3.21	11	4.58	2.29	3.67
			DAYS.			
02	01	01	1	01	01	01
03	02	02	2	03	01	02
05	03	03	3	04	02	03
07	03	04	4	06	03	04
08	04	05	**5**	07	03	06
10	05	06	6	08	04	07
12	06	07	7	10	05	08
13	07	08	8	11	06	09
15	08	09	9	13	06	10
17	08	10	**10**	14	07	11
18	09	11	11	15	08	12
20	10	12	12	17	08	13
22	11	13	13	18	09	14
23	12	14	14	19	10	16
25	13	15	**15**	21	10	17
27	13	16	16	22	11	18
28	14	17	17	24	12	19
30	15	18	18	25	13	20
32	16	18	19	26	13	21
33	17	19	**20**	28	14	22
35	18	20	21	29	15	23
37	18	21	22	31	15	24
38	19	22	23	32	16	26
40	20	23	24	33	17	27
42	21	24	**25**	35	17	28
43	22	25	26	36	18	29
45	23	26	27	38	19	30
47	23	27	28	39	19	31
48	24	28	29	40	20	32
50	25	29	**30**	42	21	33
55	28	32	33	46	23	37
1.05	53	61	63	88	44	70
1.55	78	90	93	1.29	65	1.03

51 Dollars.

12 PER CENT.	6 PER CENT.	7 PER CENT.	YEARS.	10 PER CENT.	5 PER CENT.	8 PER CENT.
6.12	3.06	3.57	1	5.10	2.55	4.08
12.24	6.12	7.14	2	10.20	5.10	8.16
18.36	9.18	10.71	3	15.30	7.65	12.24
24.48	12.24	14.28	4	20.40	10.20	16.32
30.60	15.30	17.85	5	25.50	12.75	20.40
			MONTHS.			
51	26	30	1	43	21	34
1.02	51	60	2	85	43	68
1.53	77	89	3	1.28	64	1.02
2.04	1.02	1.19	4	1.70	85	1.36
2.55	1.28	1.49	5	2.13	1.06	1.70
3.06	1.53	1.79	**6**	2.55	1.28	2.04
3.57	1.79	2.08	7	2.98	1.49	2.38
4.08	2.04	2.38	8	3.40	1.70	2.72
4.59	2.30	2.68	9	3.83	1.91	3.06
5.10	2.55	2.98	10	4.25	2.13	3.40
5.61	2.81	3.27	11	4.68	2.34	3.74
			DAYS.			
02	01	01	1	01	01	01
03	02	02	2	03	01	02
05	03	03	3	04	02	03
07	03	04	4	06	03	05
09	04	05	**5**	07	04	06
10	05	06	6	09	04	07
12	06	07	7	10	05	08
14	07	08	8	11	06	09
15	08	09	9	13	06	10
17	09	10	**10**	14	07	11
19	09	11	11	16	08	12
20	10	12	12	17	09	14
22	11	13	13	18	09	15
24	12	14	14	20	10	16
26	13	15	**15**	21	11	17
27	14	16	16	23	11	18
29	14	17	17	24	12	19
31	15	18	18	26	13	20
32	16	19	19	27	13	22
34	17	20	**20**	28	14	23
36	18	21	21	30	15	24
37	19	22	22	31	16	25
39	20	23	23	33	16	26
41	20	24	24	34	17	27
43	21	25	**25**	35	18	28
44	22	26	26	37	18	29
46	23	27	27	38	19	31
48	24	28	28	40	20	32
49	25	29	29	41	21	33
51	26	30	**30**	43	21	34
56	28	33	33	47	23	37
1.07	53	62	63	89	45	71
1.58	79	92	93	1.31	66	1.05

52 Dollars.

12 PER CENT.	6 PER CENT.	7 PER CENT.	YEARS.	10 PER CENT.	5 PER CENT.	8 PER CENT.
6.24	3.12	3.64	1	5.20	2.60	4.16
12.48	6.24	7.28	2	10.40	5.20	8.32
18.72	9.36	10.92	3	15.60	7.80	12.48
24.96	12.48	14.56	4	20.80	10.40	16.64
31.20	15.60	18.20	5	26.00	13.00	20.80
			MONTHS.			
52	26	30	1	43	22	35
1.04	52	61	2	87	43	69
1.56	78	91	3	1.30	65	1.04
2.08	1.04	1.21	4	1.73	87	1.39
2.60	1.30	1.52	5	2.17	1.08	1.73
3.12	1.56	1.82	**6**	2.60	1.30	2.08
3.64	1.82	2.12	7	3.03	1.52	2.43
4.16	2.08	2.43	8	3.47	1.73	2.77
4.68	2.34	2.73	9	3.90	1.95	3.12
5.20	2.60	3.03	10	4.33	2.17	3.47
5.72	2.86	3.34	11	4.77	2.38	3.81
			DAYS.			
02	01	01	1	01	01	01
03	02	02	2	03	01	02
05	03	03	3	04	02	03
07	03	04	4	06	03	05
09	04	05	**5**	07	04	06
10	05	06	6	09	04	07
12	06	07	7	10	05	08
14	07	08	8	12	06	09
16	08	09	9	13	07	10
17	09	10	**10**	14	07	12
19	10	11	11	16	08	13
21	10	12	12	17	09	14
23	11	13	13	19	09	15
24	12	14	14	20	10	16
26	13	15	**15**	22	11	17
28	14	16	16	23	12	18
29	15	17	17	25	12	20
31	16	18	18	26	13	21
33	16	19	19	27	14	22
35	17	20	**20**	29	14	23
36	18	21	21	30	15	24
38	19	22	22	32	16	25
40	20	23	23	33	17	27
42	21	24	24	35	17	28
43	22	25	**25**	36	18	29
45	23	26	26	38	19	30
47	23	27	27	39	20	31
49	24	28	28	40	20	32
50	25	29	29	42	21	34
52	26	30	**30**	43	22	35
57	28	33	33	48	24	38
1.09	54	64	63	91	45	73
1.61	80	94	93	1.34	67	1.08

53 Dollars.

12 PER CENT.	6 PER CENT.	7 PER CENT.	YEARS.	10 PER CENT.	5 PER CENT.	8 PER CENT.
6.36	3.18	3.71	1	5.30	2.65	4.24
12.72	6.36	7.42	2	10.60	5.30	8.48
19.08	9.54	11.13	3	15.90	7.95	12.72
25.44	12.72	14.84	4	21.20	10.60	16.96
31.80	15.90	18.55	5	26.50	13.25	21.20
			MONTHS.			
53	27	31	1	44	22	35
1.06	53	62	2	88	44	71
1.59	80	93	3	1.33	66	1.06
2.12	1.06	1.24	4	1.77	88	1.41
2.65	1.33	1.55	5	2.21	1.10	1.77
3.18	1.59	1.86	**6**	2.65	1.33	2.12
3.71	1.86	2.16	7	3.09	1.55	2.47
4.24	2.12	2.47	8	3.53	1.77	2.83
4.77	2.39	2.78	9	3.98	1.99	3.18
5.30	2.65	3.09	10	4.42	2.21	3.53
5.83	2.92	3.40	11	4.86	2.43	3.89
			DAYS.			
02	01	01	1	01	01	01
04	02	02	2	03	01	02
05	03	03	3	04	02	04
07	04	04	4	06	03	05
09	04	05	**5**	07	04	06
11	05	06	6	09	04	07
12	06	07	7	10	05	08
14	07	08	8	12	06	09
16	08	09	9	13	07	11
18	09	10	**10**	15	07	12
19	10	11	11	16	08	13
21	11	12	12	18	09	14
23	11	13	13	19	10	15
25	12	14	14	21	10	16
27	13	15	**15**	22	11	18
28	14	16	16	24	12	19
30	15	18	17	25	13	20
32	16	19	18	27	13	21
34	17	20	19	28	14	22
35	18	21	**20**	29	15	24
37	19	22	21	31	15	25
39	19	23	22	32	16	26
41	20	24	23	34	17	27
42	21	25	24	35	18	28
44	22	26	**25**	37	18	29
46	23	27	26	38	19	31
48	24	28	27	40	20	32
49	25	29	28	41	21	33
51	26	30	29	43	21	34
53	27	31	**30**	44	22	35
58	29	34	33	48	24	39
1.11	56	65	63	92	46	74
1.64	82	96	93	1.36	68	1.09

54 Dollars.

12 PER CENT.	6 PER CENT.	7 PER CENT.	YEARS.	10 PER CENT.	5 PER CENT.	8 PER CENT.
6.48	3.24	3.78	1	5:40	2.70	4.32
12.96	6.48	7.56	2	10.80	5.40	8.64
19.44	9.72	11.34	3	16.20	8.10	12.96
25.92	12.96	15.12	4	21.60	10.80	17.28
32.40	16.20	18.90	5	27.00	13.50	21.60
			MONTHS.			
54	27	32	1	45	23	36
1.08	54	63	2	90	45	72
1.62	81	95	3	1.35	68	1.08
2.16	1.08	1.26	4	1.80	90	1.44
2.70	1.35	1.58	5	2.25	1.13	1.80
3.24	1.62	1.89	**6**	2.70	1.35	2.16
3.78	1.89	2.21	7	3.15	1.58	2.52
4.32	2.16	2.52	8	3.60	1.80	2.88
4.86	2.43	2.84	9	4.05	2.03	3.24
5.40	2.70	3.15	10	4.50	2.25	3.60
5.94	2.97	3.47	11	4.95	2.48	3.96
			DAYS.			
02	01	01	1	02	01	01
04	02	02	2	03	02	02
05	03	03	3	05	02	04
07	04	04	4	06	03	05
09	05	05	**5**	08	04	06
11	05	06	6	09	05	07
13	06	07	7	11	05	08
14	07	08	8	12	06	10
16	08	09	9	14	07	11
18	09	11	**10**	15	08	12
20	10	12	11	17	08	13
22	11	13	12	18	09	14
23	12	14	13	20	10	16
25	13	15	14	21	11	17
27	14	16	**15**	23	11	18
29	14	17	16	24	12	19
31	15	18	17	26	13	20
32	16	19	18	27	14	22
34	17	20	19	29	14	23
36	18	21	**20**	30	15	24
38	19	22	21	32	16	25
40	20	23	22	33	17	26
41	21	24	23	35	17	28
43	22	25	24	36	18	29
45	23	26	**25**	38	19	30
47	23	27	26	39	20	31
49	24	28	27	41	20	32
50	25	29	28	42	21	34
52	26	30	29	44	22	35
54	27	32	**30**	45	23	36
59	29	35	33	49	25	40
1.13	56	66	63	94	47	76
1.67	83	98	93	1.39	70	1.12

55 Dollars.

12 PER CENT.	6 PER CENT.	7 PER CENT.	YEARS.	10 PER CENT.	5 PER CENT.	8 PER CENT.
6.60	3.30	3.85	1	5.50	2.75	4.40
13.20	6.60	7.70	2	11.00	5.50	8.80
19.80	9.90	11.55	3	16.50	8.25	13.20
26.40	13.20	15.40	4	22.00	11.00	17.60
33.00	16.50	19.25	5	27.50	13.75	22.00
			MONTHS.			
55	28	32	1	46	23	37
1.10	55	64	2	92	46	73
1.65	83	96	3	1.38	69	1.10
2.20	1.10	1.28	4	1.83	92	1.47
2.75	1.38	1.60	5	2.29	1.15	1.83
3.30	1.65	1.93	**6**	2.75	1.38	2.20
3.85	1.93	2.25	7	3.21	1.60	2.57
4.40	2.20	2.57	8	3.67	1.83	2.93
4.95	2.48	2.89	9	4.13	2.06	3.30
5.50	2.75	3.21	10	4.58	2.29	3.67
6.05	3.03	3.53	11	5.04	2.52	4.03
			DAYS.			
02	01	01	1	02	01	01
04	02	02	2	03	02	02
06	03	03	3	05	02	04
07	04	04	4	06	03	05
09	05	05	**5**	08	04	06
11	06	06	6	09	05	07
13	06	07	7	11	05	09
15	07	09	8	12	06	10
17	08	10	9	14	07	11
18	09	11	**10**	15	08	12
20	10	12	11	17	08	13
22	11	13	12	18	09	15
24	12	14	13	20	10	16
26	13	15	14	21	11	17
28	14	16	**15**	23	11	18
29	15	17	16	24	12	20
31	16	18	17	26	13	21
33	17	19	18	28	14	22
35	17	20	19	29	15	23
37	18	21	**20**	31	15	24
39	19	22	21	32	16	26
40	20	24	22	34	17	27
42	21	25	23	35	18	28
44	22	26	24	37	18	29
46	23	27	**25**	38	19	31
48	24	28	26	40	20	32
50	25	29	27	41	21	33
51	26	30	28	43	21	34
53	27	31	29	44	22	35
55	28	32	**30**	46	23	37
61	30	35	33	50	25	40
1.16	57	67	63	96	48	77
1.71	85	99	93	1.42	71	1.14

56 Dollars.

12 PER CENT.	6 PER CENT.	7 PER CENT.	YEARS.	10 PER CENT.	5 PER CENT.	8 PER CENT.
6.72	3.36	3.92	1	5.60	2.80	4.48
13.44	6.72	7.84	2	11.20	5.60	8.96
20.16	10.08	11.76	3	16.80	8.40	13.44
26.88	13.44	15.68	4	22.40	11.20	17.92
33.60	16.80	19.60	5	28.00	14.00	22.40
			MONTHS.			
56	28	33	1	47	23	37
1.12	56	65	2	93	47	75
1.68	84	98	3	1.40	70	1.12
2.24	1.12	1.31	4	1.87	93	1.49
2.80	1.40	1.63	5	2.33	1.17	1.87
3.36	1.68	1.96	**6**	2.80	1.40	2.24
3.92	1.96	2.29	7	3.27	1.63	2.61
4.48	2.24	2.61	8	3.73	1.87	2.99
5.04	2.52	2.94	9	4.20	2.10	3.36
5.60	2.80	3.27	10	4.67	2.33	3.73
6.16	3.08	3.59	11	5.13	2.57	4.11
			DAYS.			
02	01	01	1	02	01	01
04	02	02	2	03	02	02
06	03	03	3	05	02	04
07	04	04	4	06	03	05
09	05	05	**5**	08	04	06
11	06	07	6	09	05	07
13	07	08	7	11	05	09
15	07	09	8	12	06	10
17	08	10	9	14	07	11
19	09	11	**10**	16	08	12
21	10	12	11	17	09	14
22	11	13	12	19	09	15
24	12	14	13	20	10	16
26	13	15	14	22	11	17
28	14	16	**15**	23	12	19
30	15	17	16	25	12	20
32	16	19	17	26	13	21
34	17	20	18	28	14	22
35	18	21	19	30	15	24
37	19	22	**20**	31	16	25
39	20	23	21	33	16	26
41	21	24	22	34	17	27
43	21	25	23	36	18	29
45	22	26	24	37	19	30
47	23	27	**25**	39	19	31
49	24	28	26	40	20	32
50	25	29	27	42	21	34
52	26	30	28	44	22	35
54	27	32	29	45	23	36
56	28	33	**30**	47	23	37
62	31	36	33	51	26	41
1.18	57	69	63	98	49	78
1.74	87	1.01	93	1.44	72	1.15

57 Dollars.

12 PER CENT.	6 PER CENT.	7 PER CENT.	YEARS.	10 PER CENT.	5 PER CENT.	8 PER CENT.
6.84	3.42	3.99	1	5.70	2.85	4.56
13.68	6.84	7.98	2	11.40	5.70	9.12
20.52	10.26	11.97	3	17.10	8.55	13.68
27.36	13.68	15.96	4	22.80	11.40	18.24
34.20	17.10	19.95	5	28.50	14.25	22.80
			MONTHS.			
57	29	33	1	48	24	38
1.14	57	66	2	95	48	76
1.71	86	1.00	3	1.43	71	1.14
2.28	1.14	1.33	4	1.90	95	1.52
2.85	1.43	1.66	5	2.38	1.19	1.90
3.42	1.71	2.00	**6**	2.85	1.43	2.28
3.99	2.00	2.33	7	3.33	1.66	2.66
4.56	2.28	2.66	8	3.80	1.90	3.04
5.13	2.57	2.99	9	4.28	2.14	3.42
5.70	2.85	3.33	10	4.75	2.38	3.80
6.27	3.14	3.66	11	5.23	2.61	4.18
			DAYS.			
02	01	01	1	02	01	01
04	02	02	2	03	02	03
06	03	03	3	05	02	04
08	04	04	4	06	03	05
10	05	06	**5**	08	04	06
11	06	07	6	10	05	08
13	07	08	7	11	06	09
15	08	09	8	13	06	10
17	09	10	9	14	07	11
19	10	11	**10**	16	08	13
21	10	12	11	17	09	14
23	11	13	12	19	10	15
25	12	14	13	21	10	16
27	13	16	14	22	11	18
29	14	17	**15**	24	12	19
30	15	18	16	25	13	20
32	16	19	17	27	13	22
34	17	20	18	29	14	23
36	18	21	19	30	15	24
38	19	22	**20**	32	16	25
40	20	23	21	33	17	27
42	21	24	22	35	17	28
44	22	25	23	36	18	29
46	23	27	24	38	19	30
47	24	28	**25**	40	20	32
49	25	29	26	41	21	33
51	26	30	27	43	21	34
53	27	31	28	44	22	35
55	28	32	29	46	23	37
57	29	33	**30**	48	24	38
63	31	37	33	52	26	42
1.20	60	70	63	1.00	50	80
1.77	88	1.03	93	1.47	74	1.18

58 Dollars.

12 PER CENT.	6 PER CENT.	7 PER CENT.	YEARS.	10 PER CENT.	5 PER CENT.	8 PER CENT.
6.96	3.48	4.06	1	5.80	2.90	4.64
13.92	6.96	8.12	2	11.60	5.80	9.28
20.88	10.44	12.18	3	17.40	8.70	13.92
27.84	13.92	16.24	4	23.20	11.60	18.56
34.80	17.40	20.30	5	29.00	14.50	23.20
			MONTHS.			
58	29	34	1	48	24	39
1.16	58	68	2	97	48	77
1.74	87	1.02	3	1.45	73	1.16
2.32	1.16	1.35	4	1.93	97	1.55
2.90	1.45	1.69	5	2.42	1.21	1.93
3.48	1.74	2.03	**6**	2.90	1.45	2.32
4.06	2.03	2.37	7	3.38	1.69	2.71
4.64	2.32	2.71	8	3.87	1.93	3.09
5.22	2.61	3.05	9	4.35	2.18	3.48
5.80	2.90	3.38	10	4.83	2.42	3.87
6.38	3.19	3.72	11	5.32	2.66	4.25
			DAYS.			
02	01	01	1	02	01	01
04	02	02	2	03	02	03
06	03	03	3	05	02	04
08	04	05	4	06	03	05
10	05	06	**5**	08	04	06
12	06	07	6	10	05	08
14	07	08	7	11	06	09
15	08	09	8	13	06	10
17	09	10	9	15	07	12
19	10	11	**10**	16	08	13
21	11	12	11	18	09	14
23	12	14	12	19	10	15
25	13	15	13	21	10	17
27	14	16	14	23	11	18
29	15	17	**15**	24	12	19
31	15	18	16	26	13	21
33	16	19	17	27	14	22
35	17	20	18	29	15	23
37	18	21	19	31	15	24
39	19	23	**20**	32	16	26
41	20	24	21	34	17	27
43	21	25	22	35	18	28
44	22	26	23	37	19	30
46	23	27	24	39	19	31
48	24	28	**25**	40	20	32
50	25	29	26	42	21	34
52	26	30	27	44	22	35
54	27	32	28	45	23	36
56	28	33	29	47	23	37
58	29	34	**30**	48	24	39
63	32	37	33	53	26	43
1.21	61	71	63	1.01	51	82
1.79	90	1.05	93	1.49	75	1.21

59 Dollars.

12 PER CENT.	6 PER CENT.	7 PER CENT.	YEARS.	10 PER CENT.	5 PER CENT.	8 PER CENT.
7.08	3.54	4.13	1	5.90	2.95	4.72
14.16	7.08	8.26	2	11.80	5.90	9.44
21.24	10.62	12.39	3	17.70	8.85	14.16
28.32	14.16	16.52	4	23.60	11.80	18.88
35.40	17.70	20.65	5	29.50	14.75	23.60
			MONTHS.			
59	30	34	1	49	25	39
1.18	59	69	2	98	49	79
1.77	89	1.03	3	1.48	74	1.18
2.36	1.18	1.38	4	1.97	98	1.57
2.95	1.48	1.72	5	2.46	1.23	1.97
3.54	1.77	2.07	**6**	2.95	1.48	2.36
4.13	2.07	2.41	7	3.44	1.72	2.75
4.72	2.36	2.75	8	3.93	1.97	3.15
5.31	2.66	3.10	9	4.43	2.21	3.54
5.90	2.95	3.44	10	4.92	2.46	3.93
6.49	3.25	3.79	11	5.41	2.70	4.33
			DAYS.			
02	01	01	1	02	01	01
04	02	02	2	03	02	03
06	03	03	3	05	02	04
08	04	05	4	07	03	05
10	05	06	**5**	08	04	07
12	06	07	6	10	05	08
14	07	08	7	11	06	09
16	08	09	8	13	07	10
18	09	10	9	15	07	12
20	10	11	**10**	16	08	13
22	11	13	11	18	09	14
24	12	14	12	20	10	16
26	13	15	13	21	11	17
28	14	16	14	23	11	18
30	15	17	**15**	24	12	20
31	16	18	16	26	13	21
33	17	20	17	28	14	22
35	18	21	18	30	15	24
37	19	22	19	31	16	25
39	20	23	**20**	33	16	26
41	21	24	21	34	17	28
43	22	25	22	36	18	29
45	23	26	23	38	19	30
47	24	28	24	39	20	31
49	25	29	**25**	41	20	33
51	26	30	26	43	21	34
53	27	31	27	44	22	35
55	28	32	28	46	23	37
57	29	33	29	48	24	38
59	30	34	**30**	49	25	39
65	32	38	33	54	27	43
1.23	62	72	63	1.03	52	82
1.83	92	1.07	93	1.52	76	1.22

60 Dollars.

12 PER CENT.	6 PER CENT.	7 PER CENT.	YEARS.	10 PER CENT.	5 PER CENT.	8 PER CENT.
7.20	3.60	4.20	1	6.00	3.00	4.80
14.40	7.20	8.40	2	12.00	6.00	9.60
21.60	10.80	12.60	3	18.00	9.00	14.40
28.80	14.40	16.80	4	24.00	12.00	19.20
36.00	18.00	21.00	5	30.00	15.00	24.00
			MONTHS.			
60	30	35	1	50	25	40
1.20	60	70	2	1.00	50	80
1.80	90	1.05	3	1.50	75	1.20
2.40	1.20	1.40	4	2.00	1.00	1.60
3.00	1.50	1.75	5	2.50	1.25	2.00
3.60	1.80	2.10	**6**	3.00	1.50	2.40
4.20	2.10	2.45	7	3.50	1.75	2.80
4.80	2.40	2.80	8	4.00	2.00	3.20
5.40	2.70	3.15	9	4.50	2.25	3.60
6.00	3.00	3.50	10	5.00	2.50	4.00
6.60	3.30	3.85	11	5.50	2.75	4.40
			DAYS.			
02	01	01	1	02	01	01
04	02	02	2	03	02	03
06	03	04	3	05	03	04
08	04	05	4	07	03	05
10	05	06	**5**	08	04	07
12	06	07	6	10	05	08
14	07	08	7	12	06	09
16	08	09	8	13	07	11
18	09	11	9	15	08	12
20	10	12	**10**	17	08	13
22	11	13	11	18	09	15
24	12	14	12	20	10	16
26	13	15	13	22	11	17
28	14	16	14	23	12	19
30	15	18	**15**	25	13	20
32	16	19	16	27	13	21
34	17	20	17	28	14	23
36	18	21	18	30	15	24
38	19	22	19	32	16	25
40	20	23	**20**	33	17	27
42	21	25	21	35	18	28
44	22	26	22	37	18	29
46	23	27	23	38	19	31
48	24	28	24	40	20	32
50	25	29	**25**	42	21	33
52	26	30	26	43	22	35
54	27	32	27	45	23	36
56	28	33	28	47	23	37
58	29	34	29	48	24	39
60	30	35	**30**	50	25	40
66	33	39	33	55	28	44
1.26	63	74	63	1.05	53	84
1.86	93	1.09	93	1.55	78	1.24

61 Dollars.

12 PER CENT.	6 PER CENT.	7 PER CENT.	YEARS.	10 PER CENT.	5 PER CENT.	8 PER CENT.
7.32	3.66	4.27	1	6.10	3.05	4.88
14.64	7.32	8.54	2	12.20	6.10	9.76
21.96	10.98	12.81	3	18.30	9.15	14.64
29.28	14.64	17.08	4	24.40	12.20	19.52
36.60	18.30	21.35	5	30.50	15.25	24.40
			MONTHS.			
61	31	36	1	51	25	41
1.22	61	71	2	1.02	51	81
1.83	92	1.07	3	1.53	76	1.22
2.44	1.22	1.42	4	2.03	1.02	1.63
3.05	1.53	1.78	5	2.54	1.27	2.03
3.66	1.83	2.14	**6**	3.05	1.53	2.44
4.27	2.14	2.49	7	3.56	1.78	2.85
4.88	2.44	2.85	8	4.07	2.03	3.25
5.49	2.75	3.20	9	4.58	2.29	3.66
6.10	3.05	3.56	10	5.08	2.54	4.07
6.71	3.36	3.91	11	5.59	2.80	4.47
			DAYS.			
02	01	01	1	02	01	01
04	02	02	2	03	02	03
06	03	04	3	05	03	04
08	04	05	4	07	03	05
10	05	06	**5**	08	04	07
12	06	07	6	10	05	08
14	07	08	7	12	06	09
16	08	09	8	14	07	11
18	09	11	9	15	08	12
20	10	12	**10**	17	08	14
22	11	13	11	19	09	15
24	12	14	12	20	10	16
26	13	15	13	22	11	18
28	14	17	14	24	12	19
31	15	18	**15**	25	13	20
33	16	19	16	27	14	22
35	17	20	17	29	14	23
37	18	21	18	31	15	24
39	19	23	19	32	16	26
41	20	24	**20**	34	17	27
43	21	25	21	36	18	28
45	22	26	22	37	19	30
47	23	27	23	39	19	31
49	24	28	24	41	20	33
51	25	30	**25**	42	21	34
53	26	31	26	44	22	35
55	27	32	27	46	23	37
57	28	33	28	47	24	38
59	29	34	29	49	25	39
61	31	36	**30**	51	25	41
67	34	39	33	56	28	45
1.28	64	75	63	1.07	53	85
1.89	95	1.10	93	1.58	79	1.26

62 Dollars.

12 PER CENT.	6 PER CENT.	7 PER CENT.	YEARS.	10 PER CENT.	5 PER CENT.	8 PER CENT.
7.44	3.72	4.34	1	6.20	3.10	4.96
14.88	7.44	8.68	2	12.40	6.20	9.92
22.32	11.16	13.02	3	18.60	9.30	14.88
29.76	14.88	17.36	4	24.80	12.40	19.84
37.20	18.60	21.70	5	31.00	15.50	24.80
			MONTHS.			
62	31	36	1	52	26	41
1.24	62	72	2	1.03	52	83
1.86	93	1.09	3	1.55	78	1.24
2.48	1.24	1.45	4	2.07	1.03	1.65
3.10	1.55	1.81	5	2.58	1.29	2.07
3.72	1.86	2.17	**6**	3.10	1.55	2.48
4.34	2.17	2.53	7	3.62	1.81	2.89
4.96	2.48	2.89	8	4.13	2.07	3.31
5.58	2.79	3.26	9	4.65	2.33	3.72
6.20	3.10	3.62	10	5.17	2.58	4.13
6.82	3.41	3.98	11	5.68	2.84	4.55
			DAYS.			
02	01	01	1	02	01	01
04	02	02	2	03	02	03
06	03	04	3	05	03	04
08	04	05	4	07	03	06
10	05	06	**5**	09	04	07
12	06	07	6	10	05	08
14	07	08	7	12	06	10
17	08	10	8	14	07	11
19	09	11	9	16	08	12
21	10	12	**10**	17	09	14
23	11	13	11	19	09	15
25	12	14	12	21	10	17
27	13	16	13	22	11	18
29	14	17	14	24	12	19
31	16	18	**15**	26	13	21
33	17	19	16	28	14	22
35	18	20	17	29	15	23
37	19	22	18	31	16	25
39	20	23	19	33	16	26
41	21	24	**20**	34	17	28
43	22	25	21	36	18	29
45	23	27	22	38	19	30
48	24	28	23	40	20	32
50	25	29	24	41	21	33
52	26	30	**25**	43	22	34
54	27	31	26	45	22	36
56	28	33	27	47	23	37
58	29	34	28	48	24	39
60	30	35	29	50	25	40
62	31	36	**30**	52	26	41
68	34	40	33	57	28	45
1.30	65	76	63	1.08	54	86
1.92	96	1.12	93	1.60	80	1.27

63 Dollars.

12 PER CENT.	6 PER CENT.	7 PER CENT.	YEARS.	10 PER CENT.	5 PER CENT.	8 PER CENT.
7.56	3.78	4.41	1	6.30	3.15	5.04
15.12	7.56	8.82	2	12.60	6.30	10.08
22.68	11.34	13.23	3	18.90	9.45	15.12
30.24	15.12	17.64	4	25.20	12.60	20.16
37.80	18.90	22.05	5	31.50	15.75	25.20
			MONTHS.			
63	32	37	1	53	26	42
1.26	63	74	2	1.05	53	84
1.89	95	1.10	3	1.58	79	1.26
2.52	1.26	1.47	4	2.10	1.05	1.68
3.15	1.58	1.84	5	2.63	1.31	2.10
3.78	1.89	2.21	**6**	3.15	1.58	2.52
4.41	2.21	2.57	7	3.68	1.84	2.94
5.04	2.52	2.94	8	4.20	2.10	3.36
5.67	2.84	3.31	9	4.73	2.36	3.78
6.30	3.15	3.68	10	5.25	2.63	4.20
6.93	3.47	4.04	11	5.78	2.89	4.62
			DAYS.			
02	01	01	1	02	01	01
04	02	02	2	04	02	03
06	03	04	3	05	03	04
08	04	05	4	07	04	06
11	05	06	**5**	09	04	07
13	06	07	6	11	05	08
15	07	09	7	12	06	10
17	08	10	8	14	07	11
19	09	11	9	16	08	13
21	11	12	**10**	18	09	14
23	12	13	11	19	10	15
25	13	15	12	21	11	17
27	14	16	13	23	11	18
29	15	17	14	25	12	20
32	16	18	**15**	26	13	21
34	17	20	16	28	14	22
36	18	21	17	30	15	24
38	19	22	18	32	16	25
40	20	23	19	33	17	27
42	21	25	**20**	35	18	28
44	22	26	21	37	18	29
46	23	27	22	39	19	31
48	24	28	23	40	20	32
50	25	29	24	42	21	34
52	26	31	**25**	44	22	35
55	27	32	26	46	23	36
57	28	33	27	47	24	38
59	29	34	28	49	25	39
61	30	36	29	51	25	41
63	32	37	**30**	53	26	42
69	34	40	33	58	29	46
1.32	66	77	63	1.10	55	88
1.95	98	1.14	93	1.63	81	1.30

64 Dollars.

12 PER CENT.	6 PER CENT.	7 PER CENT.	YEARS.	10 PER CENT.	5 PER CENT.	8 PER CENT.
7.68	3.84	4.48	1	6.40	3.20	5.12
15.36	7.68	8.96	2	12.80	6.40	10.24
23.04	11.52	13.44	3	19.20	9.60	15.36
30.72	15.36	17.92	4	25.60	12.80	20.48
38.40	19.20	22.40	5	32.00	16.00	25.60
			MONTHS.			
64	32	37	1	53	27	43
1.28	64	75	2	1.07	53	85
1.92	96	1.12	3	1.60	80	1.28
2.56	1.28	1.49	4	2.13	1.07	1.71
3.20	1.60	1.87	5	2.67	1.33	2.13
3.84	1.92	2.24	**6**	3.20	1.60	2.56
4.48	2.24	2.61	7	3.73	1.87	2.99
5.12	2.56	2.99	8	4.27	2.13	3.41
5.76	2.88	3.36	9	4.80	2.40	3.84
6.40	3.20	3.73	10	5.33	2.67	4.27
7.04	3.52	4.11	11	5.87	2.93	4.69
			DAYS.			
02	01	01	1	02	01	01
04	02	02	2	04	02	03
06	03	04	3	05	03	04
09	04	05	4	07	04	06
11	05	06	**5**	09	04	07
13	06	07	6	11	05	09
15	07	09	7	12	06	10
17	09	10	8	14	07	11
19	10	11	9	16	08	13
21	11	12	**10**	18	09	14
23	12	14	11	20	10	16
26	13	15	12	21	11	17
28	14	16	13	23	12	18
30	15	17	14	25	12	20
32	16	19	**15**	27	13	21
34	17	20	16	28	14	23
36	18	21	17	30	15	24
38	19	22	18	32	16	26
41	20	24	19	34	17	27
43	21	25	**20**	36	18	28
45	22	26	21	37	19	30
47	23	27	22	39	20	31
49	25	29	23	41	20	33
51	26	30	24	43	21	34
53	27	31	**25**	44	22	36
55	28	32	26	46	23	37
58	29	34	27	48	24	38
60	30	35	28	50	25	40
62	31	36	29	52	26	41
64	32	37	**30**	53	27	43
70	35	41	33	59	29	47
1.34	67	78	63	1.12	56	90
1.98	99	1.16	93	1.65	83	1.32

65 Dollars.

12 PER CENT.	6 PER CENT.	7 PER CENT.	YEARS.	10 PER CENT.	5 PER CENT.	8 PER CENT.
7.80	3.90	4.55	1	6.50	3.25	5.20
15.60	7.80	9.10	2	13.00	6.50	10.40
23.40	11.70	13.65	3	19.50	9.75	15.60
31.20	15.60	18.20	4	26.00	13.00	20.80
39.00	19.50	22.75	5	32.50	16.25	26.00
			MONTHS.			
65	33	38	1	54	27	43
1.30	65	76	2	1.08	54	87
1.95	98	1.14	3	1.63	81	1.30
2.60	1.30	1.52	4	2.17	1.08	1.73
3.25	1.63	1.90	5	2.71	1.35	2.17
3.90	1.95	2.28	**6**	3.25	1.63	2.60
4.55	2.28	2.65	7	3.79	1.90	3.03
5.20	2.60	3.03	8	4.33	2.17	3.47
5.85	2.93	3.41	9	4.88	2.44	3.90
6.50	3.25	3.79	10	5.42	2.71	4.33
7.15	3.58	4.17	11	5.96	2.98	4.77
			DAYS.			
02	01	01	1	02	01	01
04	02	03	2	04	02	03
07	03	04	3	05	03	04
09	04	05	4	07	04	06
11	05	06	**5**	09	05	07
13	07	08	6	11	05	09
15	08	09	7	13	06	10
17	09	10	8	14	07	12
20	10	11	9	16	08	13
22	11	13	**10**	18	09	14
24	12	14	11	20	10	16
26	13	15	12	22	11	17
28	14	16	13	23	12	19
30	15	18	14	25	13	20
33	16	19	**15**	27	14	22
35	17	20	16	29	14	23
37	18	21	17	31	15	25
39	20	23	18	33	16	26
41	21	24	19	34	17	27
43	22	25	**20**	36	18	29
46	23	27	21	38	19	30
48	24	28	22	40	20	32
50	25	29	23	42	21	33
52	26	30	24	43	22	35
54	27	32	**25**	45	23	36
56	28	33	26	47	23	38
59	29	34	27	49	24	39
61	30	35	28	51	25	40
63	31	37	29	52	26	42
65	33	38	**30**	54	27	43
72	36	42	33	60	30	47
1.37	68	80	63	1.14	57	90
2.02	1.01	1.17	93	1.68	84	1.33

66 Dollars.

12 PER CENT.	6 PER CENT.	7 PER CENT.	YEARS.	10 PER CENT.	5 PER CENT.	8 PER CENT.
7.92	3.96	4.62	1	6.60	3.30	5.28
15.84	7.92	9.24	2	13.20	6.60	10.56
23.76	11.88	13.86	3	19.80	9.90	15.84
31.68	15.84	18.48	4	26.40	13.20	21.12
39.60	19.80	23.10	5	33.00	16.50	26.40
			MONTHS.			
66	33	39	1	55	28	44
1.32	66	77	2	1.10	55	88
1.98	99	1.16	3	1.65	83	1.32
2.64	1.32	1.54	4	2.20	1.10	1.76
3.30	1.65	1.93	5	2.75	1.38	2.20
3.96	1.98	2.31	**6**	3.30	1.65	2.64
4.62	2.31	2.70	7	3.85	1.93	3.08
5.28	2.64	3.08	8	4.40	2.20	3.52
5.94	2.97	3.47	9	4.95	2.48	3.96
6.60	3.30	3.85	10	5.50	2.75	4.40
7.26	3.63	4.24	11	6.05	3.03	4.84
			DAYS.			
02	01	01	1	02	01	01
04	02	03	2	04	02	03
07	03	04	3	06	03	04
09	04	05	4	07	04	06
11	05	06	**5**	09	05	07
13	07	08	6	11	06	09
15	08	09	7	13	06	10
18	09	10	8	15	07	12
20	10	12	9	17	08	13
22	11	13	**10**	18	09	15
24	12	14	11	20	10	16
26	13	15	12	22	11	18
29	14	17	13	24	12	19
31	15	18	14	26	13	21
33	17	19	**15**	28	14	22
35	18	21	16	29	15	23
37	19	22	17	31	16	25
40	20	23	18	33	17	26
42	21	24	19	35	17	28
44	22	26	**20**	37	18	29
46	23	27	21	39	19	31
48	24	28	22	40	20	32
51	25	30	23	42	21	34
53	26	31	24	44	22	35
55	28	32	**25**	46	23	37
57	29	33	26	48	24	38
59	30	35	27	50	25	40
62	31	36	28	51	26	41
64	32	37	29	53	27	43
66	33	39	**30**	55	28	44
73	36	42	33	60	30	48
1.39	69	81	63	1.15	58	92
2.05	1.02	1.19	93	1.70	85	1.36

67 Dollars.

12 PER CENT.	6 PER CENT.	7 PER CENT.	YEARS.	10 PER CENT.	5 PER CENT.	8 PER CENT.
8.04	4.02	4.69	1	6.70	3.35	5.36
16.08	8.04	9.38	2	13.40	6.70	10.72
24.12	12.06	14.07	3	20.10	10.05	16.08
32.16	16.08	18.76	4	26.80	13.40	21.44
40.20	20.10	23.45	5	33.50	16.75	26.80
			MONTHS.			
67	34	39	1	56	28	45
1.34	67	78	2	1.12	56	89
2.01	1.01	1.17	3	1.68	84	1.34
2.68	1.34	1.56	4	2.23	1.12	1.79
3.35	1.68	1.95	5	2.79	1.40	2.23
4.02	2.01	2.35	**6**	3.35	1.68	2.68
4.69	2.35	2.74	7	3.91	1.95	3.13
5.36	2.68	3.13	8	4.47	2.23	3.57
6.03	3.02	3.52	9	5.03	2.51	4.02
6.70	3.35	3.91	10	5.58	2.79	4.47
7.37	3.69	4.30	11	6.14	3.07	4.91
			DAYS.			
02	01	01	1	02	01	01
04	02	03	2	04	02	03
07	03	04	3	06	03	04
09	04	05	4	07	04	06
11	06	07	**5**	09	05	07
13	07	08	6	11	06	09
16	08	09	7	13	07	10
18	09	10	8	15	07	12
20	10	12	9	17	08	13
22	11	13	**10**	19	09	15
25	12	14	11	20	10	16
27	13	16	12	22	11	18
29	15	17	13	24	12	19
31	16	18	14	26	13	21
34	17	20	**15**	28	14	22
36	18	21	16	30	15	24
38	19	22	17	32	16	25
40	20	23	18	34	17	27
42	21	25	19	35	18	28
45	22	26	**20**	37	19	30
47	23	27	21	39	20	31
49	25	29	22	41	20	33
51	26	30	23	43	21	34
54	27	31	24	45	22	36
56	28	33	**25**	47	23	37
58	29	34	26	48	24	39
60	30	35	27	50	25	40
63	31	36	28	52	26	42
65	32	38	29	54	27	43
67	34	39	**30**	56	28	45
74	37	43	33	61	31	49
1.41	70	82	63	1.17	59	94
2.08	1.04	1.21	93	1.73	86	1.39

68 Dollars.

12 PER CENT.	6 PER CENT.	7 PER CENT.	YEARS.	10 PER CENT.	5 PER CENT.	8 PER CENT.
8.16	4.08	4.76	1	6.80	3.40	5.44
16.32	8.16	9.52	2	13.60	6.80	10.88
24.48	12.24	14.28	3	20.40	10.20	16.32
32.64	16.32	19.04	4	27.20	13.60	21.76
40.80	20.40	23.80	5	34.00	17.00	27.20
			MONTHS.			
68	34	40	1	57	28	45
1.36	68	79	2	1.13	57	91
2.04	1.02	1.19	3	1.70	85	1.36
2.72	1.36	1.59	4	2.27	1.13	1.81
3.40	1.70	1.98	5	2.83	1.42	2.27
4.08	2.04	2.38	**6**	3.40	1.70	2.72
4.76	2.38	2.78	7	3.97	1.98	3.17
5.44	2.72	3.17	8	4.53	2.27	3.63
6.12	3.06	3.57	9	5.10	2.55	4.08
6.80	3.40	3.97	10	5.67	2.83	4.53
7.48	3.74	4.36	11	6.23	3.12	4.99
			DAYS.			
02	01	01	1	02	01	02
05	02	03	2	04	02	03
07	03	04	3	06	03	05
09	05	05	4	08	04	06
11	06	07	**5**	09	05	08
14	07	08	6	11	06	09
16	08	09	7	13	07	11
18	09	11	8	15	08	12
20	10	12	9	17	09	14
23	11	13	**10**	19	09	15
25	12	15	11	21	10	17
27	14	16	12	23	11	18
29	15	17	13	25	12	20
32	16	19	14	26	13	21
34	17	20	**15**	28	14	23
36	18	21	16	30	15	24
39	19	22	17	32	16	26
41	20	24	18	34	17	27
43	22	25	19	36	18	29
45	23	26	**20**	38	19	30
48	24	28	21	40	20	32
50	25	29	22	42	21	33
52	26	30	23	43	22	35
54	27	32	24	45	23	36
57	28	33	**25**	47	24	38
59	29	34	26	49	25	39
61	31	36	27	51	26	41
63	32	37	28	53	26	42
66	33	38	29	55	27	44
68	34	40	**30**	57	28	45
75	37	44	33	62	31	50
1.43	71	83	63	1.19	59	95
2.11	1.05	1.23	93	1.75	87	1.40

69 Dollars.

12 PER CENT.	6 PER CENT.	7 PER CENT.	YEARS.	10 PER CENT.	5 PER CENT.	8 PER CENT.
8.28	4.14	4.83	1	6.90	3.45	5.52
16.56	8.28	9.66	2	13.80	6.90	11.04
24.84	12.42	14.49	3	20.70	10.35	16.56
33.12	16.56	19.32	4	27.60	13.80	22.08
41.40	20.70	24.15	5	34.50	17.25	27.60
			MONTHS.			
69	35	40	1	58	29	46
1.38	69	81	2	1.15	58	92
2.07	1.04	1.21	3	1.73	86	1.38
2.76	1.38	1.61	4	2.30	1.15	1.84
3.45	1.73	2.01	5	2.88	1.44	2.30
4.14	2.07	2.42	**6**	3.45	1.73	2.76
4.83	2.42	2.82	7	4.03	2.01	3.22
5.52	2.76	3.22	8	4.60	2.30	3.68
6.21	3.11	3.62	9	5.18	2.59	4.14
6.90	3.45	4.03	10	5.75	2.88	4.60
7.59	3.80	4.43	11	6.33	3.16	5.06
			DAYS.			
02	01	01	1	02	01	02
05	02	03	2	04	02	03
07	03	04	3	06	03	05
09	05	05	4	08	04	06
12	06	07	**5**	10	05	08
14	07	08	6	12	06	09
16	08	09	7	13	07	11
18	09	11	8	15	08	12
21	10	12	9	17	09	14
23	12	13	**10**	19	10	15
25	13	15	11	21	11	17
28	14	16	12	23	12	18
30	15	17	13	25	12	20
32	16	19	14	27	13	21
35	17	20	**15**	29	14	23
37	18	21	16	31	15	25
39	20	23	17	33	16	26
41	21	24	18	35	17	28
44	22	25	19	36	18	29
46	23	27	**20**	38	19	31
48	24	28	21	40	20	32
51	25	30	22	42	21	34
53	26	31	23	44	22	35
55	28	32	24	46	23	37
58	29	34	**25**	48	24	38
60	30	35	26	50	25	40
62	31	36	27	52	26	41
64	32	38	28	54	27	43
67	33	39	29	56	28	44
69	35	40	**30**	58	29	46
76	38	44	33	63	32	51
1.45	72	85	63	1.21	60	97
2.14	1.07	1.25	93	1.78	89	1.43

70 Dollars.

12 PER CENT.	6 PER CENT.	7 PER CENT.	YEARS.	10 PER CENT.	5 PER CENT.	8 PER CENT.
8.40	4.20	4.90	1	7.00	3.50	5.60
16.80	8.40	9.80	2	14.00	7.00	11.20
25.20	12.60	14.70	3	21.00	10.50	16.80
33.60	16.80	19.60	4	28.00	14.00	22.40
42.00	21.00	24.50	5	35.00	17.50	28.00
			MONTHS.			
70	35	41	1	58	29	47
1.40	70	82	2	1.17	58	93
2.10	1.05	1.23	3	1.75	88	1.40
2.80	1.40	1.63	4	2.33	1.17	1.87
3.50	1.75	2.04	5	2.92	1.46	2.33
4.20	2.10	2.45	**6**	3.50	1.75	2.80
4.90	2.45	2.86	7	4.08	2.04	3.27
5.60	2.80	3.27	8	4.67	2.33	3.73
6.30	3.15	3.68	9	5.25	2.63	4.20
7.00	3.50	4.08	10	5.83	2.92	4.67
7.70	3.85	4.49	11	6.42	3.21	5.13
			DAYS.			
02	01	01	1	02	01	02
05	02	03	2	04	02	03
07	04	04	3	06	03	05
09	05	05	4	08	04	06
12	06	07	**5**	10	05	08
14	07	08	6	12	06	09
16	08	10	7	14	07	11
19	09	11	8	16	08	12
21	11	12	9	18	09	14
23	12	14	**10**	19	10	16
26	13	15	11	21	11	17
28	14	16	12	23	12	19
30	15	18	13	25	13	20
33	16	19	14	27	14	22
35	18	20	**15**	29	15	23
37	19	22	16	31	16	25
40	20	23	17	33	17	26
42	21	25	18	35	18	28
44	22	26	19	37	18	30
47	23	27	**20**	39	19	31
49	25	29	21	41	20	33
51	26	30	22	43	21	34
54	27	31	23	45	22	36
56	28	33	24	47	23	37
58	29	34	**25**	49	24	39
61	30	35	26	51	25	40
63	32	37	27	53	26	42
65	33	38	28	54	27	44
68	34	39	29	56	28	45
70	35	41	**30**	58	29	47
77	39	45	33	64	32	51
1.47	74	86	63	1.22	61	98
2.17	1.09	1.27	93	1.80	90	1.45

71 Dollars.

12 PER CENT.	6 PER CENT.	7 PER CENT.	YEARS.	10 PER CENT.	5 PER CENT.	8 PER CENT.
8.52	4.26	4.97	1	7.10	3.55	5.68
17.04	8.52	9.94	2	14.20	7.10	11.36
25.56	12.78	14.91	3	21.30	10.65	17.04
34.08	17.04	19.88	4	28.40	14.20	22.72
42.60	21.30	24.85	5	35.50	17.75	28.40
			MONTHS.			
71	36	41	1	59	30	47
1.42	71	83	2	1.18	59	95
2.13	1.07	1.24	3	1.78	89	1.42
2.84	1.42	1.66	4	2.37	1.18	1.89
3.55	1.78	2.07	5	2.96	1.48	2.37
4.26	2.13	2.49	**6**	3.55	1.78	2.84
4.97	2.49	2.90	7	4.14	2.07	3.31
5.68	2.84	3.31	8	4.73	2.37	3.79
6.39	3.20	3.73	9	5.33	2.66	4.26
7.10	3.55	4.14	10	5.92	2.96	4.73
7.81	3.91	4.56	11	6.51	3.25	5.21
			DAYS.			
02	01	01	1	02	01	02
05	02	03	2	04	02	03
07	04	04	3	06	03	05
09	05	05	4	08	04	06
12	06	07	**5**	10	05	08
14	07	08	6	12	06	09
17	08	10	7	14	07	11
19	09	11	8	16	08	13
21	11	12	9	18	09	14
24	12	14	**10**	20	10	16
26	13	15	11	22	11	17
28	14	17	12	24	12	19
31	15	18	13	26	13	21
33	17	19	14	28	14	22
36	18	21	**15**	30	15	24
38	19	22	16	32	16	25
40	20	23	17	34	17	27
43	21	25	18	36	18	28
45	22	26	19	37	19	30
47	24	28	**20**	39	20	32
50	25	29	21	41	21	33
52	26	30	22	43	22	35
54	27	32	23	45	23	36
57	28	33	24	47	24	38
59	30	35	**25**	49	25	39
62	31	36	26	51	26	41
64	32	37	27	53	27	43
66	33	39	28	55	28	44
69	34	40	29	57	29	46
71	36	41	**30**	59	30	47
78	39	46	33	65	32	52
1.49	75	87	63	1.24	62	99
2.20	1.10	1.28	93	1.83	92	1.46

72 Dollars.

12 PER CENT.	6 PER CENT.	7 PER CENT.		10 PER CENT.	5 PER CENT.	8 PER CENT.
			YEARS.			
8.64	4.32	5.04	1	7.20	3.60	5.76
17.28	8.64	10.08	2	14.40	7.20	11.52
25.92	12.96	15.12	3	21.60	10.80	17.28
34.56	17.28	20.16	4	28.80	14.40	23.04
43.20	21.60	25.20	5	36.00	18.00	28.80
			MONTHS.			
72	36	42	1	60	30	48
1.44	72	84	2	1.20	60	96
2.16	1.08	1.26	3	1.80	90	1.44
2.88	1.44	1.68	4	2.40	1.20	1.92
3.60	1.80	2.10	5	3.00	1.50	2.40
4.32	2.16	2.52	**6**	3.60	1.80	2.88
5.04	2.52	2.94	7	4.20	2.10	3.36
5.76	2.88	3.36	8	4.80	2.40	3.84
6.48	3.24	3.78	9	5.40	2.70	4.32
7.20	3.60	4.20	10	6.00	3.00	4.80
7.92	3.96	4.62	11	6.60	3.30	5.28
			DAYS.			
02	01	01	1	02	01	02
05	02	03	2	04	03	03
07	04	04	3	06	03	05
10	05	06	4	08	04	06
12	06	07	**5**	10	05	08
14	07	08	6	12	06	10
17	08	10	7	14	07	11
19	10	11	8	16	08	13
22	11	13	9	18	09	14
24	12	14	**10**	20	10	16
26	13	15	11	22	11	18
29	14	17	12	24	12	19
31	16	18	13	26	13	21
34	17	20	14	28	14	22
36	18	21	**15**	30	15	24
38	19	22	16	32	16	26
41	20	24	17	34	17	27
43	22	25	18	36	18	29
46	23	27	19	38	19	30
48	24	28	**20**	40	20	32
50	25	29	21	42	21	34
53	26	31	22	44	22	35
55	28	32	23	46	23	37
58	29	34	24	48	24	38
60	30	35	**25**	50	25	40
62	31	36	26	52	26	42
65	32	38	27	54	27	43
67	34	39	28	56	28	45
70	35	41	29	58	29	46
72	36	42	**30**	60	30	48
79	40	46	33	66	33	53
1.51	76	88	63	1.26	63	1.01
2.23	1.12	1.30	93	1.86	93	1.49

73 Dollars.

12 PER CENT.	6 PER CENT.	7 PER CENT,	YEARS.	10 PER CENT.	5 PER CENT.	8 PER CENT.
8.76	4.38	5.11	1	7.30	3.65	5.84
17.52	8.76	10.22	2	14.60	7.30	11.68
26.28	13.14	15.33	3	21.90	10.95	17.52
35.04	17.52	20.44	4	29.20	14.60	23.36
43.80	21.90	25.55	5	36.50	18.25	29.20
			MONTHS.			
73	37	43	1	61	30	49
1.46	73	85	2	1.22	61	97
2.19	1.10	1.28	3	1.83	91	1.46
2.92	1.46	1.70	4	2.43	1.22	1.95
3.65	1.83	2.13	5	3.04	1.52	2.43
4.38	2.19	2.56	**6**	3.65	1.83	2.92
5.11	2.56	2.98	7	4.26	2.13	3.41
5.84	2.92	3.41	8	4.87	2.43	3.89
6.57	3.29	3.83	9	5.48	2.74	4.38
7.30	3.65	4.26	10	6.08	3.04	4.87
8.03	4.02	4.68	11	6.69	3.35	5.35
			DAYS.			
02	01	01	1	02	01	02
05	02	03	2	04	02	03
07	04	04	3	06	03	05
10	05	06	4	08	04	06
12	06	07	**5**	10	05	08
15	07	09	6	12	06	10
17	09	10	7	14	07	11
19	10	11	8	16	08	13
22	11	13	9	18	09	15
24	12	14	**10**	20	10	16
27	13	16	11	22	11	18
29	15	17	12	24	12	19
32	16	18	13	26	13	21
34	17	20	14	28	14	23
37	18	21	**15**	30	15	24
39	19	23	16	32	16	26
41	21	24	17	34	17	28
44	22	26	18	37	18	29
46	23	27	19	39	19	31
49	24	28	**20**	41	20	32
51	26	30	21	43	21	34
54	27	31	22	45	22	36
56	28	33	23	47	23	37
58	29	34	24	49	24	39
61	30	35	**25**	51	25	41
63	32	37	26	53	26	42
66	33	38	27	55	27	44
68	34	40	28	57	28	45
71	35	41	29	59	29	47
73	37	43	**30**	61	30	49
80	40	47	33	67	33	54
1.53	77	89	63	1.28	64	1.02
2.26	1.13	1.32	93	1.89	94	1.51

74 Dollars.

12 PER CENT.	6 PER CENT.	7 PER CENT.	YEARS.	10 PER CENT.	5 PER CENT.	8 PER CENT.
8.88	4.44	5.18	1	7.40	3.70	5.92
17.76	8.88	10.36	2	14.80	7.40	11.84
26.64	13.32	15.54	3	22.20	11.10	17.76
35.52	17.76	20.72	4	29.60	14.80	23.68
44.40	22.20	25.90	5	37.00	18.50	29.60
			MONTHS.			
74	37	43	1	62	31	49
1.48	74	86	2	1.23	62	99
2.22	1.11	1.30	3	1.85	93	1.48
2.96	1.48	1.73	4	2.47	1.23	1.97
3.70	1.85	2.16	5	3.08	1.54	2.47
4.44	2.22	2.59	**6**	3.70	1.85	2.96
5.18	2.59	3.02	7	4.32	2.16	3.45
5.92	2.96	3.45	8	4.93	2.47	3.95
6.66	3.33	3.89	9	5.55	2.78	4.44
7.40	3.70	4.32	10	6.17	3.08	4.93
8.14	4.07	4.75	11	6.78	3.39	5.43
			DAYS.			
02	01	01	1	02	01	02
05	02	03	2	04	02	03
07	04	04	3	06	03	05
10	05	06	4	08	04	07
12	06	07	**5**	10	05	08
15	07	09	6	12	06	10
17	09	10	7	14	07	12
20	10	12	8	16	08	13
22	11	13	9	19	09	15
25	12	14	**10**	21	10	16
27	14	16	11	23	11	18
30	15	17	12	25	12	20
32	16	19	13	27	13	21
35	17	20	14	29	14	23
37	19	22	**15**	31	15	25
39	20	23	16	33	16	26
42	21	24	17	35	17	28
44	22	26	18	37	19	30
47	23	27	19	39	20	31
49	25	29	**20**	41	21	33
52	26	30	21	43	22	35
54	27	32	22	45	23	36
57	28	33	23	47	24	38
59	30	35	24	49	25	39
62	31	36	**25**	51	26	41
64	32	37	26	53	27	43
67	33	39	27	56	28	44
69	35	40	28	58	29	46
72	36	42	29	60	30	48
74	37	43	**30**	62	31	49
81	41	47	33	68	34	54
1.55	78	91	63	1.29	65	1.03
2.29	1.15	1.34	93	1.91	96	1.52

75 Dollars.

12 PER CENT.	6 PER CENT.	7 PER CENT,	YEARS.	10 PER CENT.	5 PER CENT.	8 PER CENT.
9.00	4.50	5.25	1	7.50	3.75	6.00
18.00	9.00	10.50	2	15.00	7.50	12.00
27.00	13.50	15.75	3	22.50	11.25	18.00
36.00	18.00	21.00	4	30.00	15.00	24.00
45.00	22.50	26.25	5	37.50	18.75	30.00
			MONTHS.			
75	38	44	1	63	31	50
1.50	75	88	2	1.25	63	1.00
2.25	1.13	1.31	3	1.88	94	1.50
3.00	1.50	1.75	4	2.50	1.25	2.00
3.75	1.88	2.19	5	3.13	1.56	2.50
4.50	2.25	2.63	**6**	3.75	1.88	3.00
5.25	2.63	3.06	7	4.38	2.19	3.50
6.00	3.00	3.50	8	5.00	2.50	4.00
6.75	3.38	3.94	9	5.63	2.81	4.50
7.50	3.75	4.38	10	6.25	3.13	5.00
8.25	4.13	4.81	11	6.88	3.44	5.50
			DAYS.			
03	01	01	1	02	01	02
05	03	03	2	04	02	03
08	04	04	3	06	03	05
10	05	06	4	08	04	07
13	06	07	**5**	10	05	08
15	08	09	6	13	06	10
18	09	10	7	15	07	12
20	10	12	8	17	08	13
23	11	13	9	19	09	15
25	13	15	**10**	21	10	17
28	14	16	11	23	11	18
30	15	18	12	25	13	20
33	16	19	13	27	14	22
35	18	20	14	29	15	23
38	19	22	**15**	31	16	25
40	20	23	16	33	17	27
43	21	25	17	35	18	28
45	23	26	18	38	19	30
48	24	28	19	40	20	32
50	25	29	**20**	42	21	33
53	26	31	21	44	22	35
55	28	32	22	46	23	37
58	29	34	23	48	24	38
60	30	35	24	50	25	40
63	31	36	**25**	52	26	42
65	33	38	26	54	27	43
68	34	39	27	56	28	45
70	35	41	28	58	29	47
73	36	42	29	60	30	48
75	38	44	**30**	63	31	50
83	41	48	33	69	34	55
1.58	79	92	63	1.31	66	1.05
2.33	1.16	1.36	93	1.94	97	1.55

76 Dollars.

12 PER CENT.	6 PER CENT.	7 PER CENT.	YEARS.	10 PER CENT.	5 PER CENT.	8 PER CENT.
9.12	4.56	5.32	1	7.60	3.80	6.08
18.24	9.12	10.64	2	15.20	7.60	12.16
27.36	13.68	15.96	3	22.80	11.40	18.24
36.48	18.24	21.28	4	30.40	15.20	24.32
45.60	22.80	26.60	5	38.00	19.00	30.40
			MONTHS.			
76	38	44	1	63	32	51
1.52	76	89	2	1.27	63	1.01
2.28	1.14	1.33	3	1.90	95	1.52
3.04	1.52	1.77	4	2.53	1.27	2.03
3.80	1.90	2.22	5	3.17	1.58	2.53
4.56	2.28	2.66	**6**	3.80	1.90	3.04
5.32	2.66	3.10	7	4.43	2.22	3.55
6.08	3.04	3.55	8	5.07	2.53	4.05
6.84	3.42	3.99	9	5.70	2.85	4.56
7.60	3.80	4.43	10	6.33	3.17	5.07
8.36	4.18	4.88	11	6.97	3.48	5.57
			DAYS.			
03	01	01	1	02	01	02
05	03	03	2	04	02	03
08	04	04	3	06	03	05
10	05	06	4	08	04	07
13	06	07	**5**	11	05	08
15	08	09	6	13	06	10
18	09	10	7	15	07	12
20	10	12	8	17	08	14
23	11	13	9	19	10	15
25	13	15	**10**	21	11	17
28	14	16	11	23	12	19
30	15	18	12	25	13	20
33	16	19	13	27	14	22
35	18	21	14	30	15	24
38	19	22	**15**	32	16	25
41	20	24	16	34	17	27
43	22	25	17	36	18	29
46	23	27	18	38	19	30
48	24	28	19	40	20	32
51	25	30	**20**	42	21	34
53	27	31	21	44	22	35
56	28	33	22	46	23	37
58	29	34	23	49	24	39
61	30	35	24	51	25	41
63	32	37	**25**	53	26	42
66	33	38	26	55	27	44
68	34	40	27	57	29	46
71	35	41	28	59	30	47
73	37	43	29	61	31	49
76	38	44	**30**	63	32	51
84	42	49	33	70	35	56
1.60	80	93	63	1.33	66	1.06
2.36	1.18	1.37	93	1.96	98	1.57

77 Dollars.

12 PER CENT.	6 PER CENT.	7 PER CENT,	YEARS.	10 PER CENT.	5 PER CENT.	8 PER CENT.
9.24	4.62	5.39	1	7.70	3.85	6.16
18.48	9.24	10.78	2	15.40	7.70	12.32
27.72	13.86	16.17	3	23.10	11.55	18.48
36.96	18.48	21.56	4	30.80	15.40	24.64
46.20	23.10	26.95	5	38.50	19.25	30.80
			MONTHS.			
77	39	45	1	64	32	51
1.54	77	90	2	1.28	64	1.03
2.31	1.16	1.35	3	1.93	96	1.54
3.08	1.54	1.80	4	2.57	1.28	2.05
3.85	1.93	2.25	5	3.21	1.60	2.57
4.62	2.31	2.70	**6**	3.85	1.93	3.08
5.39	2.70	3.14	7	4.49	2.25	3.59
6.16	3.08	3.59	8	5.13	2.57	4.11
6.93	3.47	4.04	9	5.78	2.89	4.62
7.70	3.85	4.49	10	6.42	3.21	5.13
8.47	4.24	4.94	11	7.06	3.53	5.65
			DAYS.			
03	01	01	1	02	01	02
05	03	03	2	04	02	03
08	04	04	3	06	03	05
10	05	06	4	09	04	07
13	06	07	**5**	11	05	09
15	08	09	6	13	06	10
18	09	10	7	15	07	12
21	10	12	8	17	09	14
23	12	13	9	19	10	15
26	13	15	**10**	21	11	17
28	14	16	11	24	12	19
31	15	18	12	26	13	21
33	17	19	13	28	14	22
36	18	21	14	30	15	24
39	19	22	**15**	32	16	26
41	21	24	16	34	17	27
44	22	25	17	36	18	29
46	23	27	18	39	19	31
49	24	28	19	41	20	33
51	26	30	**20**	43	21	34
54	27	31	21	45	22	36
56	28	33	22	47	24	38
59	30	34	23	49	25	39
62	31	36	24	51	26	41
64	32	37	**25**	53	27	43
67	33	39	26	56	28	44
69	35	40	27	58	29	46
72	36	42	28	60	30	48
74	37	43	29	62	31	50
77	39	45	**30**	64	32	51
85	42	49	33	71	35	56
1.62	81	94	63	1.35	67	1.07
2.39	1.19	1.39	93	1.99	99	1.59

78 Dollars.

12 PER CENT.	6 PER CENT.	7 PER CENT.	YEARS.	10 PER CENT.	5 PER CENT.	8 PER CENT.
9.36	4.68	5.46	1	7.80	3.90	6.24
18.72	9.36	10.92	2	15.60	7.80	12.48
28.08	14.04	16.38	3	23.40	11.70	18.72
37.44	18.72	21.84	4	31.20	15.60	24.96
46.80	23.40	27.30	5	39.00	19.50	31.20
			MONTHS.			
78	39	46	1	65	33	52
1.56	78	91	2	1.30	65	1.04
2.34	1.17	1.37	3	1.95	98	1.56
3.12	1.56	1.82	4	2.60	1.30	2.08
3.90	1.95	2.28	5	3.25	1.63	2.60
4.68	2.34	2.73	**6**	3.90	1.95	3.12
5.46	2.73	3.19	7	4.55	2.28	3.64
6.24	3.12	3.64	8	5.20	2.60	4.16
7.02	3.51	4.10	9	5.85	2.93	4.68
7.80	3.90	4.55	10	6.50	3.25	5.20
8.58	4.29	5.01	11	7.15	3.58	5.72
			DAYS.			
03	01	02	1	02	01	02
05	03	03	2	04	02	03
08	04	05	3	07	03	05
10	05	06	4	09	04	07
13	06	08	**5**	11	05	09
16	08	09	6	13	07	10
18	09	11	7	15	08	12
21	10	12	8	17	09	14
23	12	14	9	20	10	16
26	13	15	**10**	22	11	17
29	14	17	11	24	12	19
31	16	18	12	26	13	21
34	17	20	13	28	14	23
36	18	21	14	30	15	24
39	20	23	**15**	33	16	26
42	21	24	16	35	17	28
44	22	26	17	37	18	29
47	23	27	18	39	20	31
49	25	29	19	41	21	33
52	26	30	**20**	43	22	35
55	27	32	21	46	23	36
57	29	33	22	48	24	38
60	30	35	23	50	25	40
62	31	36	24	52	26	42
65	33	38	**25**	54	27	43
68	34	39	26	56	28	45
70	35	41	27	59	29	47
73	36	42	28	61	30	49
75	38	44	29	63	31	50
78	39	46	**30**	65	33	52
86	43	50	33	71	36	57
1.64	82	96	63	1.36	68	1.09
2.42	1.21	1.41	93	2.01	1.01	1.61

79 Dollars.

12 PER CENT.	6 PER CENT.	7 PER CENT.	YEARS.	10 PER CENT.	5 PER CENT.	8 PER CENT.
9.48	4.74	5.53	1	7.90	3.95	6.32
18.96	9.48	11.06	2	15.80	7.90	12.64
28.44	14.22	16.59	3	23.70	11.85	18.96
37.92	18.96	22.12	4	31.60	15.80	25.28
47.40	23.70	27.65	5	39.50	19.75	31.60
			MONTHS.			
79	40	46	1	66	33	53
1.58	79	92	2	1.32	66	1.05
2.37	1.19	1.38	3	1.98	99	1.58
3.16	1.58	1.84	4	2.63	1.32	2.11
3.95	1.98	2.30	5	3.29	1.65	2.63
4.74	2.37	2.77	**6**	3.95	1.98	3.16
5.53	2.77	3.23	7	4.61	2.30	3.69
6.32	3.16	3.69	8	5.27	2.63	4.21
7.11	3.56	4.15	9	5.93	2.96	4.74
7.90	3.95	4.61	10	6.58	3.29	5.27
8.69	4.35	5.07	11	7.24	3.62	5.79
			DAYS.			
03	01	02	1	02	01	02
05	03	03	2	04	02	04
08	04	05	3	07	03	05
11	05	06	4	09	04	07
13	07	08	**5**	11	05	09
16	08	09	6	13	07	11
18	09	11	7	15	08	12
21	11	12	8	18	09	14
24	12	14	9	20	10	16
26	13	15	**10**	22	11	18
29	14	17	11	24	12	19
32	16	18	12	26	13	21
34	17	20	13	29	14	23
37	18	22	14	31	15	25
40	20	23	**15**	33	16	26
42	21	25	16	35	18	28
45	22	26	17	37	19	30
47	24	28	18	40	20	32
50	25	29	19	42	21	33
53	26	31	**20**	44	22	35
55	28	32	21	46	23	37
58	29	34	22	48	24	39
61	30	35	23	50	25	40
63	32	37	24	53	26	42
66	33	38	**25**	55	27	44
68	34	40	26	57	29	46
71	36	41	27	59	30	47
74	37	43	28	61	31	49
76	38	45	29	64	32	51
79	40	46	**30**	66	33	53
87	43	51	33	72	36	58
1.66	83	97	63	1.38	69	1.11
2.45	1.23	1.43	93	2.04	1.02	1.63

80 Dollars.

12 PER CENT.	6 PER CENT.	7 PER CENT.	YEARS.	10 PER CENT.	5 PER CENT.	8 PER CENT.
9.60	4.80	5.60	1	8.00	4.00	6.40
19.20	9.60	11.20	2	16.00	8.00	12.80
28.80	14.40	16.80	3	24.00	12.00	19.20
38.40	19.20	22.40	4	32.00	16.00	25.60
48.00	24.00	28.00	5	40.00	20.00	32.00
			MONTHS.			
80	40	47	1	67	33	53
1.60	80	93	2	1.33	67	1.07
2.40	1.20	1.40	3	2.00	1.00	1.60
3.20	1.60	1.87	4	2.67	1.33	2.13
4.00	2.00	2.33	5	3.33	1.67	2.67
4.80	2.40	2.80	**6**	4.00	2.00	3.20
5.60	2.80	3.27	7	4.67	2.33	3.73
6.40	3.20	3.73	8	5.33	2.67	4.27
7.20	3.60	4.20	9	6.00	3.00	4.80
8.00	4.00	4.67	10	6.67	3.33	5.33
8.80	4.40	5.13	11	7.33	3.67	5.87
			DAYS.			
03	01	02	1	02	01	02
05	03	03	2	04	02	04
08	04	05	3	07	03	05
11	05	06	4	09	04	07
13	07	08	**5**	11	06	09
16	08	09	6	13	07	11
19	09	11	7	16	08	12
21	11	12	8	18	09	14
24	12	14	9	20	10	16
27	13	16	**10**	22	11	18
29	15	17	11	24	12	20
32	16	19	12	27	13	21
35	17	20	13	29	14	23
37	19	22	14	31	16	25
40	20	23	**15**	33	17	27
43	21	25	16	36	18	28
45	23	26	17	38	19	30
48	24	28	18	40	20	32
51	25	30	19	42	21	34
53	27	31	**20**	44	22	36
56	28	33	21	47	23	37
59	29	34	22	49	24	39
61	31	36	23	51	26	41
64	32	37	24	53	27	43
67	33	39	**25**	56	28	44
69	35	40	26	58	29	46
72	36	42	27	60	30	48
75	37	44	28	62	31	50
77	39	45	29	64	32	52
80	40	47	**30**	67	33	53
88	44	51	33	73	37	59
1.68	84	98	63	1.40	70	1.12
2.48	1.24	1.45	93	2.07	1.03	1.65

81 Dollars.

12 PER CENT.	6 PER CENT.	7 PER CENT.	YEARS.	10 PER CENT.	5 PER CENT.	8 PER CENT.
9.72	4.86	5.67	1	8.10	4.05	6.48
19.44	9.72	11.34	2	16.20	8.10	12.96
29.16	14.58	17.01	3	24.30	12.15	19.44
38.88	19.44	22.68	4	32.40	16.20	25.92
48.60	24.30	28.35	5	40.50	20.25	32.40
			MONTHS.			
81	41	47	1	68	34	54
1.62	81	95	2	1.35	68	1.08
2.43	1.22	1.42	3	2.03	1.01	1.62
3.24	1.62	1.89	4	2.70	1.35	2.16
4.05	2.03	2.36	5	3.38	1.69	2.70
4.86	2.43	2.84	**6**	4.05	2.03	3.24
5.67	2.84	3.31	7	4.73	2.36	3.78
6.48	3.24	3.78	8	5.40	2.70	4.32
7.29	3.65	4.25	9	6.08	3.04	4.86
8.10	4.05	4.73	10	6.75	3.38	5.40
8.91	4.46	5.20	11	7.43	3.71	5.94
			DAYS.			
03	01	02	1	02	01	02
05	03	03	2	04	02	04
08	04	05	3	07	03	05
11	05	06	4	09	04	07
14	07	08	**5**	11	06	09
16	08	09	6	14	07	11
19	09	11	7	16	08	13
22	11	13	8	18	09	14
24	12	14	9	20	10	16
27	14	16	**10**	23	11	18
30	15	17	11	25	12	20
32	16	19	12	27	14	22
35	18	20	13	29	15	23
38	19	22	14	32	16	25
41	20	24	**15**	34	17	27
43	22	25	16	36	18	29
46	23	27	17	38	19	31
49	24	28	18	41	20	32
51	26	30	19	43	21	34
54	27	32	**20**	45	23	36
57	28	33	21	47	24	38
59	30	35	22	50	25	40
62	31	36	23	52	26	41
65	32	38	24	54	27	43
67	34	39	**25**	56	28	45
70	35	41	26	59	29	47
73	36	43	27	61	30	49
76	38	44	28	63	32	50
78	39	46	29	65	33	52
81	41	47	**30**	68	34	54
89	44	52	33	74	37	59
1.70	85	99	63	1.42	71	1.13
2.51	1.26	1.46	93	2.09	1.05	1.67

82 Dollars.

12 PER CENT.	6 PER CENT.	7 PER CENT.	YEARS.	10 PER CENT.	5 PER CENT.	8 PER CENT.
9.84	4.92	5.74	1	8.20	4.10	6.56
19.68	9.84	11.48	2	16.40	8.20	13.12
29.52	14.76	17.22	3	24.60	12.30	19.68
39.36	19.68	22.96	4	32.80	16.40	26.24
49.20	24.60	28.70	5	41.00	20.50	32.80
			MONTHS.			
82	41	48	1	68	34	55
1.64	82	96	2	1.37	68	1.09
2.46	1.23	1.44	3	2.05	1.03	1.64
3.28	1.64	1.91	4	2.73	1.37	2.19
4.10	2.05	2.39	5	3.42	1.71	2.73
4.92	2.46	2.87	**6**	4.10	2.05	3.28
5.74	2.87	3.35	7	4.78	2.39	3.83
6.56	3.28	3.83	8	5.47	2.73	4.37
7.38	3.69	4.31	9	6.15	3.08	4.92
8.20	4.10	4.78	10	6.83	3.42	5.47
9.02	4.51	5.26	11	7.52	3.76	6.01
			DAYS.			
03	01	02	1	02	01	02
05	03	03	2	05	02	04
08	04	05	3	07	03	05
11	05	06	4	09	05	07
14	07	08	**5**	11	06	09
16	08	10	6	14	07	11
19	10	11	7	16	08	13
22	11	13	8	18	09	15
25	12	14	9	21	10	16
27	14	16	**10**	23	11	18
30	15	18	11	25	13	20
33	16	19	12	27	14	22
36	18	21	13	30	15	24
38	19	22	14	32	16	26
41	21	24	**15**	34	17	27
44	22	26	16	36	18	29
46	23	27	17	39	19	31
49	25	29	18	41	21	33
52	26	30	19	43	22	35
55	27	32	**20**	46	23	36
57	29	33	21	48	24	38
60	30	35	22	50	25	40
63	31	37	23	52	26	42
66	33	38	24	55	27	44
68	34	40	**25**	57	28	46
71	36	41	26	59	30	47
74	37	43	27	62	31	49
77	38	45	28	64	32	51
79	40	46	29	66	33	53
82	41	48	**30**	68	34	55
90	45	53	33	75	38	60
1.72	86	1.00	63	1.43	72	1.15
2.54	1.27	1.48	93	2.10	1.06	1.70

83 Dollars.

12 PER CENT.	6 PER CENT.	7 PER CENT.	YEARS.	10 PER CENT.	5 PER CENT.	8 PER CENT.
9.96	4.98	5.81	1	8.30	4.15	6.64
19.92	9.96	11.62	2	16.60	8.30	13.28
29.88	14.94	17.43	3	24.90	12.45	19.92
39.84	19.92	23.24	4	33.20	16.60	26.56
49.80	24.90	29.05	5	41.50	20.75	33.20
			MONTHS.			
83	42	48	1	69	35	55
1.66	83	97	2	1.38	69	1.11
2.49	1.25	1.45	3	2.08	1.04	1.66
3.32	1.66	1.94	4	2.77	1.38	2.21
4.15	2.08	2.42	5	3.46	1.73	2.77
4.98	2.49	2.91	**6**	4.15	2.08	3.32
5.81	2.91	3.39	7	4.84	2.42	3.87
6.64	3.32	3.87	8	5.53	2.77	4.43
7.47	3.74	4.36	9	6.23	3.11	4.98
8.30	4.15	4.84	10	6.92	3.46	5.53
9.13	4.57	5.33	11	7.61	3.80	6.09
			DAYS.			
03	01	02	1	02	01	02
06	03	03	2	05	02	04
08	04	05	3	07	03	06
11	06	06	4	09	05	07
14	07	08	**5**	12	06	09
17	08	10	6	14	07	11
19	10	11	7	16	08	13
22	11	13	8	18	09	15
25	12	15	9	21	10	17
28	14	16	**10**	23	12	18
30	15	18	11	25	13	20
33	17	19	12	28	14	22
36	18	21	13	30	15	24
39	19	23	14	32	16	26
42	21	24	**15**	35	17	28
44	22	26	16	37	18	30
47	24	27	17	39	20	31
50	25	29	18	42	21	33
53	26	31	19	44	22	35
55	28	32	**20**	46	23	37
58	29	34	21	48	24	39
61	30	36	22	51	25	41
64	32	37	23	53	27	42
66	33	39	24	55	28	44
69	35	40	**25**	58	29	46
72	36	42	26	60	30	48
75	37	44	27	62	31	50
77	39	45	28	65	32	52
80	40	47	29	67	33	53
83	42	48	**30**	69	35	55
91	45	53	33	76	38	61
1.74	87	1.02	63	1.45	73	1.16
2.57	1.29	1.50	93	2.14	1.07	1.71

84 Dollars.

12 PER CENT.	6 PER CENT.	7 PER CENT.	YEARS.	10 PER CENT.	5 PER CENT.	8 PER CENT.
10.08	5.04	5.88	1	8.40	4.20	6.72
20.16	10.08	11.76	2	16.80	8.40	13.44
30.24	15.12	17.64	3	25.20	12.60	20.16
40.32	20.16	23.52	4	33.60	16.80	26.88
50.40	25.20	29.40	5	42.00	21.00	33.60
			MONTHS.			
84	42	49	1	70	35	56
1.68	84	98	2	1.40	70	1.12
2.52	1.26	1.47	3	2.10	1.05	1.68
3.36	1.68	1.96	4	2.80	1.40	2.24
4.20	2.10	2.45	5	3.50	1.75	2.80
5.04	2.52	2.94	**6**	4.20	2.10	3.36
5.88	2.94	3.43	7	4.90	2.45	3.92
6.72	3.36	3.92	8	5.60	2.80	4.48
7.56	3.78	4.41	9	6.30	3.15	5.04
8.40	4.20	4.90	10	7.00	3.50	5.60
9.24	4.62	5.39	11	7.70	3.85	6.16
			DAYS.			
03	01	02	1	02	01	02
06	03	03	2	05	02	04
08	04	05	3	07	03	06
11	06	07	4	09	05	07
14	07	08	**5**	12	06	09
17	08	10	6	14	07	11
20	10	11	7	16	08	13
22	11	13	8	19	09	15
25	13	15	9	21	11	17
28	14	16	**10**	23	12	19
31	15	18	11	26	13	21
34	17	20	12	28	14	22
36	18	21	13	30	15	24
39	20	23	14	33	16	26
42	21	25	**15**	35	18	28
45	22	26	16	37	19	30
48	24	28	17	40	20	32
50	25	29	18	42	21	34
53	27	31	19	44	22	35
56	28	33	**20**	47	23	37
59	29	34	21	49	25	39
62	31	36	22	51	26	41
64	32	38	23	54	27	43
67	34	39	24	56	28	45
70	35	41	**25**	58	29	47
73	36	42	26	61	30	49
76	38	44	27	63	32	50
78	39	46	28	65	33	52
81	41	47	29	68	34	54
84	42	49	**30**	70	35	56
92	46	54	33	77	38	62
1.76	88	1.03	63	1.47	73	1.18
2.60	1.30	1.52	93	2.17	1.08	1.74

85 Dollars.

12 PER CENT.	6 PER CENT.	7 PER CENT.	YEARS.	10 PER CENT.	5 PER CENT.	8 PER CENT.
10.20	5.10	5.95	1	8.50	4.25	6.80
20.40	10.20	11.90	2	17.00	8.50	13.60
30.60	15.30	17.85	3	25.50	12.75	20.40
40.80	20.40	23.80	4	34.00	17.00	27.20
51.00	25.50	29.75	5	42.50	21.25	34.00
			MONTHS.			
85	43	50	1	71	35	57
1.70	85	99	2	1.42	71	1.13
2.55	1.28	1.49	3	2.13	1.06	1.70
3.40	1.70	1.98	4	2.83	1.42	2.27
4.25	2.13	2.48	5	3.54	1.77	2.83
5.10	2.55	2.98	**6**	4.25	2.13	3.40
5.95	2.98	3.47	7	4.96	2.48	3.97
6.80	3.40	3.97	8	5.67	2.83	4.53
7.65	3.83	4.46	9	6.38	3.19	5.10
8.50	4.25	4.96	10	7.08	3.54	5.67
9.35	4.68	5.45	11	7.79	3.90	6.23
			DAYS.			
03	01	02	1	02	01	02
06	03	03	2	05	02	04
09	04	05	3	07	04	06
11	06	07	4	09	05	08
14	07	08	**5**	12	06	09
17	09	10	6	14	07	11
20	10	12	7	17	08	13
23	11	13	8	19	09	15
26	13	15	9	21	11	17
28	14	17	**10**	24	12	19
31	16	18	11	26	13	21
34	17	20	12	28	14	23
37	18	21	13	31	15	25
40	20	23	14	33	17	26
43	21	25	**15**	35	18	28
45	23	26	16	38	19	30
48	24	28	17	40	20	32
51	26	30	18	43	21	34
54	27	31	19	45	22	36
57	28	33	**20**	47	24	38
60	30	35	21	50	25	40
62	31	36	22	52	26	42
65	33	38	23	54	27	43
68	34	40	24	57	28	45
71	35	41	**25**	59	30	47
74	37	43	26	61	31	49
77	38	45	27	64	32	51
79	40	46	28	66	33	53
82	41	48	29	68	34	55
85	43	50	**30**	71	35	57
94	47	55	33	78	39	63
1.79	89	1.04	63	1.49	74	1.20
2.64	1.32	1.54	93	2.19	1.10	1.77

86 Dollars.

12 PER CENT.	6 PER CENT.	7 PER CENT.	YEARS.	10 PER CENT.	5 PER CENT.	8 PER CENT.
10.32	5.16	6.02	1	8.60	4.30	6.88
20.64	10.32	12.04	2	17.20	8.60	13.76
30.96	15.48	18.06	3	25.80	12.90	20.64
41.28	20.64	24.08	4	34.40	17.20	27.52
51.60	25.80	30.10	5	43.00	21.50	34.40
			MONTHS.			
86	43	50	1	72	36	57
1.72	86	1.00	2	1.43	72	1.15
2.58	1.29	1.51	3	2.15	1.08	1.72
3.44	1.72	2.01	4	2.87	1.43	2.29
4.30	2.15	2.51	5	3.58	1.79	2.87
5.16	2.58	3.01	**6**	4.30	2.15	3.44
6.02	3.01	3.51	7	5.02	2.51	4.01
6.88	3.44	4.01	8	5.73	2.87	4.59
7.74	3.87	4.52	9	6.45	3.23	5.16
8.60	4.30	5.02	10	7.17	3.58	5.73
9.46	4.73	5.52	11	7.88	3.94	6.31
			DAYS.			
03	01	02	1	02	01	02
06	03	03	2	05	02	04
09	04	05	3	07	04	06
11	06	07	4	10	05	08
14	07	08	**5**	12	06	10
17	09	10	6	14	07	11
20	10	12	7	17	08	13
23	11	13	8	19	10	15
26	13	15	9	22	11	17
29	14	17	**10**	24	12	19
32	16	18	11	26	13	21
34	17	20	12	29	14	23
37	19	22	13	31	16	25
40	20	23	14	33	17	27
43	22	25	**15**	36	18	29
46	23	27	16	38	19	31
49	24	28	17	41	20	32
52	26	30	18	43	22	34
54	27	32	19	45	23	36
57	29	33	**20**	48	24	38
60	30	35	21	50	25	40
63	32	37	22	53	26	42
66	33	38	23	55	27	44
69	34	40	24	57	29	46
72	36	42	**25**	60	30	48
75	37	43	26	62	31	50
77	39	45	27	65	32	52
80	40	47	28	67	33	54
83	42	48	29	69	35	55
86	43	50	**30**	72	36	57
95	47	55	33	79	39	63
1.81	90	1.05	63	1.50	75	1.20
2.67	1.33	1.55	93	2.22	1.11	1.77

87 Dollars.

12 PER CENT.	6 PER CENT.	7 PER CENT,	YEARS.	10 PER CENT.	5 PER CENT.	8 PER CENT.
10.44	5.22	6.09	1	8.70	4.35	6.96
20.88	10.44	12.18	2	17.40	8.70	13.92
31.32	15.66	18.27	3	26.10	13.05	20.88
41.76	20.88	24.36	4	34.80	17.40	27.84
52.20	26.10	30.45	5	43.50	21.75	34.80
			MONTHS.			
87	44	51	1	73	36	58
1.74	87	1.02	2	1.45	73	1.16
2.61	1.31	1.52	3	2.18	1.09	1.74
3.48	1.74	2.03	4	2.90	1.45	2.32
4.35	2.18	2.54	5	3.63	1.81	2.90
5.22	2.61	3.05	**6**	4.35	2.18	3.48
6.09	3.05	3.55	7	5.08	2.54	4.06
6.96	3.48	4.06	8	5.80	2.90	4.64
7.83	3.92	4.57	9	6.53	3.26	5.22
8.70	4.35	5.08	10	7.25	3.63	5.80
9.57	4.79	5.58	11	7.98	3.99	6.38
			DAYS.			
03	01	02	1	02	01	02
06	03	03	2	05	02	04
09	04	05	3	07	04	06
12	06	07	4	10	05	08
15	07	08	**5**	12	06	10
17	09	10	6	15	07	12
20	10	12	7	17	08	14
23	12	14	8	19	10	15
26	13	15	9	22	11	17
29	15	17	**10**	24	12	19
32	16	19	11	27	13	21
35	17	20	12	29	15	23
38	19	22	13	31	16	25
41	20	24	14	34	17	27
44	22	25	**15**	36	18	29
46	23	27	16	39	19	31
49	25	29	17	41	21	33
52	26	30	18	44	22	35
55	28	32	19	46	23	37
58	29	34	**20**	48	24	39
61	30	36	21	51	25	41
64	32	37	22	53	27	43
67	33	39	23	56	28	44
70	35	41	24	58	29	46
73	36	42	**25**	60	30	48
75	38	44	26	63	31	50
78	39	46	27	65	33	52
81	41	47	28	68	34	54
84	42	49	29	70	35	56
87	44	51	**30**	73	36	58
96	48	56	33	80	40	64
1.83	92	1.07	63	1.52	76	1.22
2.70	1.35	1.57	93	2.25	1.12	1.80

88 Dollars.

12 PER CENT.	6 PER CENT.	7 PER CENT.	YEARS.	10 PER CENT.	5 PER CENT.	8 PER CENT.
10.56	5.28	6.16	1	8.80	4.40	7.04
21.12	10.56	12.32	2	17.60	8.80	14.08
31.68	15.84	18.48	3	26.40	13.20	21.12
42.24	21.12	24.64	4	35.20	17.60	28.16
52.80	26.40	30.80	5	44.00	22.00	35.20
			MONTHS.			
88	44	51	1	73	37	59
1.76	88	1.03	2	1.47	73	1.17
2.64	1.32	1.54	3	2.20	1.10	1.76
3.52	1.76	2.05	4	2.93	1.47	2.35
4.40	2.20	2.57	5	3.67	1.83	2.93
5.28	2.64	3.08	**6**	4.40	2.20	3.52
6.16	3.08	3.59	7	5.13	2.57	4.11
7.04	3.52	4.11	8	5.87	2.93	4.69
7.92	3.96	4.62	9	6.60	3.30	5.28
8.80	4.40	5.13	10	7.33	3.67	5.87
9.68	4.84	5.65	11	8.07	4.03	6.45
			DAYS.			
03	01	02	1	02	01	02
06	03	03	2	05	02	04
09	04	05	3	07	04	06
12	06	07	4	10	05	08
15	07	09	**5**	12	06	10
18	09	10	6	15	07	12
21	10	12	7	17	09	14
23	12	14	8	20	10	16
26	13	15	9	22	11	18
29	15	17	**10**	24	12	20
32	16	19	11	27	13	22
35	18	21	12	29	15	23
38	19	22	13	32	16	25
41	21	24	14	34	17	27
44	22	26	**15**	37	18	29
47	23	27	16	39	20	31
50	25	29	17	42	21	33
53	26	31	18	44	22	35
56	28	33	19	46	23	37
59	29	34	**20**	49	24	39
62	31	36	21	51	26	41
65	32	38	22	54	27	43
67	34	39	23	56	28	45
70	35	41	24	59	29	47
73	37	43	**25**	61	31	49
76	38	44	26	64	32	51
79	40	46	27	66	33	53
82	41	48	28	68	34	55
85	43	50	29	71	35	57
88	44	51	**30**	73	37	59
97	48	56	33	80	40	65
1.85	92	1.08	63	1.53	77	1.24
2.73	1.36	1.59	93	2.27	1.14	1.83

89 Dollars.

12 PER CENT.	6 PER CENT.	7 PER CENT.	YEARS.	10 PER CENT.	5 PER CENT.	8 PER CENT.
10.68	5.34	6.23	1	8.90	4.45	7.12
21.36	10.68	12.46	2	17.80	8.90	14.24
32.04	16.02	18.69	3	26.70	13.35	21.36
42.72	21.36	24.92	4	35.60	17.80	28.48
53.40	26.70	31.15	5	44.50	22.25	35.60
			MONTHS.			
89	45	52	1	74	37	59
1.78	89	1.04	2	1.48	74	1.19
2.67	1.34	1.56	3	2.23	1.11	1.78
3.56	1.78	2.08	4	2.97	1.48	2.37
4.45	2.23	2.60	5	3.71	1.85	2.97
5.34	2.67	3.12	**6**	4.45	2.23	3.56
6.23	3.12	3.63	7	5.19	2.60	4.15
7.12	3.56	4.15	8	5.93	2.97	4.75
8.01	4.01	4.67	9	6.68	3.34	5.34
8.90	4.45	5.19	10	7.42	3.71	5.93
9.79	4.90	5.71	11	8.16	4.08	6.53
			DAYS.			
03	01	02	1	02	01	02
06	03	03	2	05	02	04
09	04	05	3	07	04	06
12	06	07	4	10	05	08
15	07	09	**5**	12	06	10
18	09	10	6	15	07	12
21	10	12	7	17	09	14
24	12	14	8	20	10	16
27	13	16	9	22	11	18
30	15	17	**10**	25	12	20
33	16	19	11	27	14	22
36	18	21	12	30	15	24
39	19	22	13	32	16	26
42	21	24	14	35	17	28
45	22	26	**15**	37	19	30
47	24	28	16	40	20	32
50	25	29	17	42	21	34
53	27	31	18	45	22	36
56	28	33	19	47	23	38
59	30	35	**20**	49	25	40
62	31	36	21	52	26	42
65	33	38	22	54	27	44
68	34	40	23	57	28	45
71	36	42	24	59	30	47
74	37	43	**25**	62	31	49
77	39	45	26	64	32	51
80	40	47	27	67	33	53
83	42	48	28	69	35	55
86	43	50	29	72	36	57
89	45	52	**30**	74	37	59
98	49	57	33	81	41	65
1.87	93	1.09	63	1.55	78	1.24
2.76	1.38	1.61	93	2.29	1.15	1.83

90 Dollars.

12 PER CENT.	6 PER CENT.	7 PER CENT.	YEARS.	10 PER CENT.	5 PER CENT.	8 PER CENT.
10.80	5.40	6.30	1	9.00	4.50	7.20
21.60	10.80	12.60	2	18.00	9.00	14.40
32.40	16.20	18.90	3	27.00	13.50	21.60
43.20	21.60	25.20	4	36.00	18.00	28.80
54.00	27.00	31.50	5	45.00	22.50	36.00
			MONTHS.			
90	45	53	1	75	38	60
1.80	90	1.05	2	1.50	75	1.20
2.70	1.35	1.58	3	2.25	1.13	1.80
3.60	1.80	2.10	4	3.00	1.50	2.40
4.50	2.25	2.63	5	3.75	1.88	3.00
5.40	2.70	3.15	**6**	4.50	2.25	3.60
6.30	3.15	3.68	7	5.25	2.63	4.20
7.20	3.60	4.20	8	6.00	3.00	4.80
8.10	4.05	4.73	9	6.75	3.38	5.40
9.00	4.50	5.25	10	7.50	3.75	6.00
9.90	4.95	5.78	11	8.25	4.13	6.60
			DAYS.			
03	02	02	1	03	01	02
06	03	04	2	05	03	04
09	05	05	3	08	04	06
12	06	07	4	10	05	08
15	08	09	**5**	13	06	10
18	09	11	6	15	08	12
21	11	12	7	18	09	14
24	12	14	8	20	10	16
27	14	16	9	23	11	18
30	15	18	**10**	25	13	20
33	17	19	11	28	14	22
36	18	21	12	30	15	24
39	20	23	13	33	16	26
42	21	25	14	35	18	28
45	23	26	**15**	38	19	30
48	24	28	16	40	20	32
51	26	30	17	43	21	34
54	27	32	18	45	23	36
57	29	33	19	48	24	38
60	30	35	**20**	50	25	40
63	32	37	21	53	26	42
66	33	39	22	55	28	44
69	35	40	23	58	29	46
72	36	42	24	60	30	48
75	38	44	**25**	63	31	50
78	39	46	26	65	33	52
81	41	47	27	68	34	54
84	42	49	28	70	35	56
87	44	51	29	73	36	58
90	45	53	**30**	75	38	60
99	50	58	33	83	41	66
1.89	95	1.11	63	1.58	79	1.26
2.79	1.40	1.64	93	2.33	1.16	1.86

91 Dollars.

12 PER CENT.	6 PER CENT.	7 PER CENT.	YEARS.	10 PER CENT.	5 PER CENT.	8 PER CENT.
10.92	5.46	6.37	1	9.10	4.55	7.28
21.84	10.92	12.74	2	18.20	9.10	14.56
32.76	16.38	19.11	3	27.30	13.65	21.84
43.68	21.84	25.48	4	36.40	18.20	29.12
54.60	27.30	31.85	5	45.50	22.75	36.40
			MONTHS.			
91	46	53	1	76	38	61
1.82	91	1.06	2	1.52	76	1.21
2.73	1.37	1.59	3	2.28	1.14	1.82
3.64	1.82	2.12	4	3.03	1.52	2.43
4.55	2.28	2.65	5	3.79	1.90	3.03
5.46	2.73	3.19	**6**	4.55	2.28	3.64
6.37	3.19	3.72	7	5.31	2.65	4.25
7.28	3.64	4.25	8	6.07	3.03	4.85
8.19	4.10	4.78	9	6.83	3.41	5.46
9.10	4.55	5.31	10	7.58	3.79	6.07
10.01	5.01	5.84	11	8.34	4.17	6.67
			DAYS.			
03	02	02	1	03	01	02
06	03	04	2	05	03	04
09	05	05	3	08	04	06
12	06	07	4	10	05	08
15	08	09	**5**	13	06	10
18	09	11	6	15	08	12
21	11	12	7	18	09	14
24	12	14	8	20	10	16
27	14	16	9	23	11	18
30	15	18	**10**	25	13	20
33	17	19	11	28	14	22
36	18	21	12	30	15	24
39	20	23	13	33	16	26
42	21	25	14	35	18	28
46	23	27	**15**	38	19	30
49	24	28	16	40	20	32
52	26	30	17	43	21	34
55	27	32	18	46	23	36
58	29	34	19	48	24	38
61	30	35	**20**	51	25	40
64	32	37	21	53	27	42
67	33	39	22	56	28	44
70	35	41	23	58	29	47
73	36	42	24	61	30	49
76	38	44	**25**	63	32	51
79	39	46	26	66	33	53
82	41	48	27	68	34	55
85	42	50	28	71	35	57
88	44	51	29	73	37	59
91	46	53	**30**	76	38	61
1.00	50	58	33	83	42	67
1.91	96	1.11	63	1.59	80	1.27
2.82	1.41	1.65	93	2.35	1.17	1.88

92 Dollars.

12 PER CENT.	6 PER CENT.	7 PER CENT.	YEARS.	10 PER CENT.	5 PER CENT.	8 PER. CENT.
11.04	5.52	6.44	1	9.20	4.60	7.36
22.08	11.04	12.88	2	18.40	9.20	14.72
33.12	16.56	19.32	3	27.60	13.80	22.08
44.16	22.08	25.76	4	36.80	18.40	29.44
55.20	27.60	32.20	5	46.00	23.00	36.80
			MONTHS.			
92	46	54	1	77	38	61
1.84	92	1.07	2	1.53	77	1.23
2.76	1.38	1.61	3	2.30	1.15	1.84
3.68	1.84	2.15	4	3.07	1.53	2.45
4.60	2.30	2.68	5	3.83	1.92	3.07
5.52	2.76	3.22	**6**	4.60	2.30	3.68
6.44	3.22	3.76	7	5.37	2.68	4.29
7.36	3.68	4.29	8	6.13	3.07	4.91
8.28	4.14	4.83	9	6.90	3.45	5.52
9.20	4.60	5.37	10	7.67	3.83	6.13
10.12	5.06	5.90	11	8.43	4.22	6.75
			DAYS.			
03	02	02	1	03	01	02
06	03	04	2	05	03	04
09	05	05	3	08	04	06
12	06	07	4	10	05	08
15	08	09	**5**	13	06	10
18	09	11	6	15	08	12
21	11	13	7	18	09	14
25	12	14	8	20	10	16
28	14	16	9	23	12	18
31	15	18	**10**	26	13	20
34	17	20	11	28	14	22
37	18	21	12	31	15	25
40	20	23	13	33	17	27
43	21	25	14	36	18	29
46	23	27	**15**	38	19	31
49	25	29	16	41	20	33
52	26	30	17	43	22	35
55	28	32	18	46	23	37
58	29	34	19	49	24	39
61	31	36	**20**	51	26	41
64	32	38	21	54	27	43
67	34	39	22	56	28	45
71	35	41	23	59	29	47
74	37	43	24	61	31	49
77	38	45	**25**	64	32	51
80	40	47	26	66	33	53
83	41	48	27	69	35	55
86	43	50	28	72	36	57
89	44	52	29	74	37	59
92	46	54	**30**	77	38	61
1.01	50	59	33	84	42	67
1.93	96	1.13	63	1.61	81	1.28
2.85	1.42	1.66	93	2.38	1.19	1.90

93 Dollars.

12 PER CENT.	6 PER CENT.	7 PER CENT,	YEARS.	10 PER CENT.	5 PER CENT.	8 PER CENT.
11.16	5.58	6.51	1	9.30	4.65	7.44
22.32	11.16	13.02	2	18.60	9.30	14.88
33.48	16.74	19.53	3	27.90	13.95	22.32
44.64	22.32	26.04	4	37.20	18.60	29.76
55.80	27.90	32.55	5	46.50	23.25	37.20
			MONTHS.			
93	47	54	1	78	39	62
1.86	93	1.09	2	1.55	78	1.24
2.79	1.40	1.63	3	2.33	1.16	1.86
3.72	1.86	2.17	4	3.10	1.55	2.48
4.65	2.33	2.71	5	3.88	1.94	3.10
5.58	2.79	3.26	**6**	4.65	2.33	3.72
6.51	3.26	3.80	7	5.43	2.71	4.34
7.44	3.72	4.34	8	6.20	3.10	4.96
8.37	4.19	4.88	9	6.98	3.49	5.58
9.30	4.65	5.43	10	7.75	3.88	6.20
10.23	5.12	5.97	11	8.53	4.26	6.82
			DAYS.			
03	02	02	1	03	01	02
06	03	04	2	05	03	04
09	05	05	3	08	04	06
12	06	07	4	10	05	08
15	08	09	**5**	13	06	10
19	09	11	6	16	08	12
22	11	13	7	18	09	14
25	12	14	8	21	10	17
28	14	16	9	23	12	19
31	16	18	**10**	26	13	21
34	17	20	11	28	14	23
37	19	22	12	31	16	25
40	20	24	13	34	17	27
43	22	25	14	36	18	29
47	23	27	**15**	39	19	31
50	25	29	16	41	21	33
53	26	31	17	44	22	35
56	28	33	18	47	23	37
59	29	34	19	49	25	39
62	31	36	**20**	52	26	41
65	33	38	21	54	27	43
68	34	40	22	57	28	45
71	36	42	23	59	30	48
74	37	43	24	62	31	50
77	39	45	**25**	65	32	52
81	40	47	26	67	34	54
84	42	49	27	70	35	56
87	43	51	28	72	36	58
90	45	52	29	75	37	60
93	47	54	**30**	78	39	62
1.02	51	60	33	85	43	68
1.95	98	1.14	63	1.63	81	1.30
2.88	1.44	1.68	93	2.40	1.20	1.92

94 Dollars.

12 PER CENT.	6 PER CENT.	7 PER CENT.	YEARS.	10 PER CENT.	5 PER CENT.	8 PER CENT.
11.28	5.64	6.58	1	9.40	4.70	7.52
22.56	11.28	13.16	2	18.80	9.40	15.04
33.84	16.92	19.74	3	28.20	14.10	22.56
45.12	22.56	26.32	4	37.60	18.80	30.08
56.40	28.20	32.90	5	47.00	23.50	37.60
			MONTHS.			
94	47	55	1	78	39	63
1.88	94	1.10	2	1.57	78	1.25
2.82	1.41	1.65	3	2.35	1.18	1.88
3.76	1.88	2.19	4	3.13	1.57	2.51
4.70	2.35	2.74	5	3.92	1.96	3.13
5.64	2.82	3.29	**6**	4.70	2.35	3.76
6.58	3.29	3.84	7	5.48	2.74	4.39
7.52	3.76	4.39	8	6.27	3.13	5.01
8.46	4.23	4.94	9	7.05	3.53	5.64
9.40	4.70	5.48	10	7.83	3.92	6.27
10.34	5.17	6.03	11	8.62	4.31	6.89
			DAYS.			
03	02	02	1	03	01	02
06	03	04	2	05	03	04
09	05	05	3	08	04	06
13	06	07	4	10	05	08
16	08	09	**5**	13	07	10
19	09	11	6	16	08	13
22	11	13	7	18	09	15
25	13	15	8	21	10	17
28	14	16	9	24	12	19
31	16	18	**10**	26	13	21
34	17	20	11	29	14	23
38	19	22	12	31	16	25
41	20	24	13	34	17	27
44	22	26	14	37	18	29
47	24	27	**15**	39	20	31
50	25	29	16	42	21	33
53	27	31	17	44	22	36
56	28	33	18	47	24	38
60	30	35	19	50	25	40
63	31	37	**20**	52	26	42
66	33	38	21	55	27	44
69	34	40	22	57	29	46
72	36	42	23	60	30	48
75	38	44	24	63	31	50
78	39	46	**25**	65	33	52
81	41	48	26	68	34	54
85	42	49	27	71	35	56
88	44	51	28	73	37	58
91	45	53	29	76	38	61
94	47	55	**30**	78	39	63
1.03	51	60	33	86	43	69
1.97	98	1.15	63	1.64	82	1.32
2.91	1.45	1.70	93	2.43	1.21	1.95

95 Dollars.

12 PER CENT.	6 PER CENT.	7 PER CENT.	YEARS.	10 PER CENT.	5 PER CENT.	8 PER CENT.
11.40	5.70	6.65	1	9.50	4.75	7.60
22.80	11.40	13.30	2	19.00	9.50	15.20
34.20	17.10	19.95	3	28.50	14.25	22.80
45.60	22.80	26.60	4	38.00	19.00	30.40
57.00	28.50	33.25	5	47.50	23.75	38.00
			MONTHS.			
95	48	55	1	79	40	63
1.90	95	1.11	2	1.58	79	1.27
2.85	1.43	1.66	3	2.38	1.19	1.90
3.80	1.90	2.22	4	3.17	1.58	2.53
4.75	2.38	2.77	5	3.96	1.98	3.17
5.70	2.85	3.33	**6**	4.75	2.38	3.80
6.65	3.33	3.88	7	5.54	2.77	4.43
6.70	3.80	4.43	8	6.33	3.17	5.07
8.55	4.28	4.99	9	7.13	3.56	5.70
9.50	4.75	5.54	10	7.92	3.96	6.33
10.45	5.23	6.10	11	8.71	4.35	6.97
			DAYS.			
03	02	02	1	03	01	02
06	03	04	2	05	03	04
10	05	06	3	08	04	06
13	06	07	4	11	05	08
16	08	09	**5**	13	07	11
19	10	11	6	16	08	13
22	11	13	7	18	09	15
25	13	15	8	21	11	17
29	14	17	9	24	12	19
32	16	18	**10**	26	13	21
35	17	20	11	29	15	23
38	19	22	12	32	16	25
41	21	24	13	34	17	27
44	22	26	14	37	18	30
48	24	28	**15**	40	20	32
51	25	30	16	42	21	34
54	27	31	17	45	22	36
57	29	33	18	48	24	38
60	30	35	19	50	25	40
63	32	37	**20**	53	26	42
67	33	39	21	55	28	44
70	35	41	22	58	29	46
73	36	42	23	61	30	49
76	38	44	24	63	32	51
79	40	46	**25**	66	33	53
82	41	48	26	69	34	55
86	43	50	27	71	36	57
89	44	52	28	74	37	59
92	46	54	29	77	38	61
95	48	55	**30**	79	40	63
1.04	52	61	33	87	43	69
1.99	1.00	1.16	63	1.66	83	1.33
2.94	1.47	1.72	93	2.45	1.23	1.96

96 Dollars.

12 PER CENT.	6 PER CENT.	7 PER CENT,	YEARS.	10 PER CENT.	5 PER CENT.	8 PER CENT.
11.52	5.76	6.72	1	9.60	4.80	7.68
23.04	11.52	13.44	2	19.20	9.60	15.36
34.56	17.28	20.16	3	28.80	14.40	23.04
46.08	23.04	26.88	4	38.40	19.20	30.72
57.60	28.80	33.60	5	48.00	24.00	38.40
			MONTHS.			
96	48	56	1	80	40	64
1.92	96	1.12	2	1.60	80	1.28
2.88	1.44	1.68	3	2.40	1.20	1.92
3.84	1.92	2.24	4	3.20	1.60	2.56
4.80	2.40	2.80	5	4.00	2.00	3.20
5.76	2.88	3.36	**6**	4.80	2.40	3.84
6.72	3.36	3.92	7	5.60	2.80	4.48
7.68	3.84	4.48	8	6.40	3.20	5.12
8.64	4.32	5.04	9	7.20	3.60	5.76
9.60	4.80	5.60	10	8.00	4.00	6.40
10.56	5.28	6.16	11	8.80	4.40	7.04
			DAYS.			
03	02	02	1	03	01	02
06	03	04	2	05	03	04
10	05	06	3	08	04	06
13	06	07	4	11	05	09
16	08	09	**5**	13	07	11
19	10	11	6	16	08	13
22	11	13	7	19	09	15
26	13	15	8	21	11	17
29	14	17	9	24	12	19
32	16	19	**10**	27	13	21
35	18	21	11	29	15	23
38	19	22	12	32	16	26
42	21	24	13	35	17	28
45	22	26	14	37	19	30
48	24	28	**15**	40	20	32
51	26	30	16	43	21	34
54	27	32	17	45	23	36
58	29	34	18	48	24	38
61	30	35	19	51	25	41
64	32	37	**20**	53	27	43
67	34	39	21	56	28	45
70	35	41	22	59	29	47
74	37	43	23	61	31	49
77	38	45	24	64	32	51
80	40	47	**25**	67	33	53
83	42	49	26	69	35	55
86	43	50	27	72	36	58
90	45	52	28	75	37	60
93	46	54	29	77	39	62
96	48	56	**30**	80	40	64
1.06	53	62	33	88	44	70
2.02	1.01	1.18	63	1.68	84	1.34
2.98	1.49	1.74	93	2.48	1.24	1.98

97 Dollars.

12 PER CENT.	6 PER CENT.	7 PER CENT.	YEARS.	10 PER CENT.	5 PER CENT.	8 PER CENT.
11.64	5.82	6.79	1	9.70	4.85	7.76
23.28	11.64	13.58	2	19.40	9.70	15.52
34.92	17.46	20.37	3	29.10	14.55	23.28
46.56	23.28	27.16	4	38.80	19.40	31.04
58.20	29.10	33.95	5	48.50	24.25	38.80
			MONTHS.			
97	49	57	1	81	40	65
1.94	97	1.13	2	1.62	81	1.29
2.91	1.46	1.70	3	2.43	1.21	1.94
3.88	1.94	2.26	4	3.23	1.62	2.59
4.85	2.43	2.83	5	4.04	2.02	3.23
5.82	2.91	3.40	**6**	4.85	2.43	3.88
6.79	3.40	3.96	7	5.66	2.83	4.53
7.76	3.88	4.53	8	6.47	3.23	5.17
8.73	4.37	5.09	9	7.28	3.64	5.82
9.70	4.85	5.66	10	8.08	4.04	6.47
10.67	5.34	6.22	11	8.89	4.45	7.11
			DAYS.			
03	02	02	1	03	01	02
06	03	04	2	05	03	04
10	05	06	3	08	04	06
13	06	08	4	11	05	09
16	08	09	**5**	13	07	11
19	10	11	6	16	08	13
23	11	13	7	19	09	15
26	13	15	8	22	11	17
29	15	17	9	24	12	19
32	16	19	**10**	27	13	22
36	18	21	11	30	15	24
39	19	23	12	32	16	26
42	21	25	13	35	18	28
45	23	26	14	38	19	30
49	24	28	**15**	40	20	32
52	26	30	16	43	22	34
55	27	32	17	46	23	37
58	29	34	18	49	24	39
61	31	36	19	51	26	41
65	32	38	**20**	54	27	43
68	34	40	21	57	28	45
71	36	41	22	59	30	47
74	37	43	23	62	31	50
78	39	45	24	65	32	52
81	40	47	**25**	67	34	54
84	42	49	26	70	35	56
87	44	51	27	73	36	58
91	45	53	28	75	38	60
94	47	55	29	78	39	63
97	49	57	**30**	81	40	65
1.07	53	62	33	88	44	71
2.04	1.02	1.19	63	1.70	85	1.36
3.01	1.50	1.76	93	2.50	1.25	2.01

98 Dollars.

12 PER CENT.	6 PER CENT.	7 PER CENT.	YEARS.	10 PER CENT.	5 PER CENT.	8 PER CENT.
11.76	5.88	6.86	1	9.80	4.90	7.84
23.52	11.76	13.72	2	19.60	9.80	15.68
35.28	17.64	20.58	3	29.40	14.70	23.52
47.04	23.52	27.44	4	39.20	19.60	31.36
58.80	29.40	34.30	5	49.00	24.50	39.20
			MONTHS.			
98	49	57	1	82	41	65
1.96	98	1.14	2	1.63	82	1.31
2.94	1.47	1.72	3	2.45	1.23	1.96
3.92	1.96	2.29	4	3.27	1.63	2.61
4.90	2.45	2.86	5	4.08	2.04	3.27
5.88	2.94	3.43	**6**	4.90	2.45	3.92
6.86	3.43	4.00	7	5.72	2.86	4.57
7.84	3.92	4.57	8	6.53	3.27	5.23
8.82	4.41	5.15	9	7.35	3.68	5.88
9.80	4.90	5.72	10	8.17	4.08	6.53
10.78	5.39	6.29	11	8.98	4.49	7.19
			DAYS.			
03	02	02	1	03	01	02
07	03	04	2	05	03	04
10	05	06	3	08	04	07
13	07	08	4	11	05	09
16	08	10	**5**	14	07	11
20	10	11	6	16	08	13
23	11	13	7	19	10	15
26	13	15	8	22	11	17
29	15	17	9	25	12	20
33	16	19	**10**	27	14	22
36	18	21	11	30	15	24
39	20	23	12	33	16	26
42	21	25	13	35	18	28
46	23	27	14	38	19	30
49	25	29	**15**	41	20	33
52	26	30	16	44	22	35
56	28	32	17	46	23	37
59	29	34	18	49	25	39
62	31	36	19	52	26	41
65	33	38	**20**	54	27	44
69	34	40	21	57	29	46
72	36	42	22	60	30	48
75	38	44	23	63	31	50
78	39	46	24	65	33	52
81	41	48	**25**	68	34	54
85	42	50	26	71	35	57
88	44	51	27	74	37	59
91	46	53	28	76	38	61
95	47	55	29	79	39	63
98	49	57	**30**	82	41	65
1.08	54	63	33	90	45	72
2.06	1.03	1.20	63	1.71	85	1.37
3.04	1.52	1.77	93	2.53	1.26	2.02

99 Dollars.

12 PER CENT.	6 PER CENT.	7 PER CENT.	YEARS.	10 PER CENT.	5 PER CENT	8 PER CENT.
11.88	5.94	6.93	1	9.90	4.95	7.92
23.76	11.88	13.86	2	19.80	9.90	15.84
35.64	17.82	20.79	3	29.70	14.85	23.76
47.52	23.76	27.72	4	39.60	19.80	31.68
59.40	29.70	34.65	5	49.50	24.75	39.60
			MONTHS.			
99	50	58	1	83	41	66
1.98	99	1.16	2	1.65	83	1.32
2.97	1.49	1.73	3	2.48	1.24	1.98
3.96	1.98	2.31	4	3.30	1.65	2.64
4.95	2.48	2.89	5	4.13	2.06	3.30
5.94	2.97	3.47	**6**	4.95	2.48	3.96
6.93	3.47	4.04	7	5.78	2.89	4.62
7.92	3.96	4.62	8	6.60	3.30	5.28
8.91	4.46	5.20	9	7.43	3.71	5.94
9.90	4.95	5.78	10	8.25	4.13	6.60
10.89	5.45	6.35	11	9.08	4.54	7.26
			DAYS.			
03	02	02	1	03	01	02
07	03	04	2	06	03	04
10	05	06	3	08	04	07
13	07	08	4	11	06	09
16	08	10	**5**	14	07	11
20	10	12	6	17	08	13
23	12	13	7	19	10	15
26	13	15	8	22	11	18
30	15	17	9	25	12	20
33	17	19	**10**	28	14	22
36	18	21	11	30	15	24
40	20	23	12	33	17	26
43	21	25	13	36	18	29
46	23	27	14	39	19	31
50	25	29	**15**	41	21	33
53	26	31	16	44	22	35
56	28	33	17	47	23	37
59	30	35	18	50	25	40
63	31	37	19	52	26	42
66	33	39	**20**	55	28	44
69	35	40	21	58	29	46
73	36	42	22	61	30	48
76	38	44	23	63	32	51
79	40	46	24	66	33	53
82	41	48	**25**	69	34	55
86	43	50	26	72	36	57
89	45	52	27	74	37	59
92	46	54	28	77	39	62
96	48	56	29	80	40	64
99	50	58	**30**	83	41	66
1.09	54	64	33	91	45	73
2.08	1.04	1.21	63	1.73	87	1.39
3.07	1.53	1.79	93	2.56	1.28	2.05

100 Dollars.

12 PER CENT.	6 PER CENT.	7 PER CENT.	YEARS.	10 PER CENT.	5 PER CENT.	8 PER CENT.
12.00	6.00	7.00	1	10.00	5.00	8.00
24.00	12.00	14.00	2	20.00	10.00	16.00
36.00	18.00	21.00	3	30.00	15.00	24.00
48.00	24.00	28.00	4	40.00	20.00	32.00
60.00	30.00	35.00	5	50.00	25.00	40.00
			MONTHS.			
1.00	50	58	1	83	42	67
2.00	1.00	1.17	2	1.67	83	1.33
3.00	1.50	1.75	3	2.50	1.25	2.00
4.00	2.00	2.33	4	3.33	1.67	2.67
5.00	2.50	2.92	5	4.17	2.08	3.33
6.00	3.00	3.50	**6**	5.00	2.50	4.00
7.00	3.50	4.08	7	5.83	2.92	4.67
8.00	4.00	4.67	8	6.67	3.33	5.33
9.00	4.50	5.25	9	7.50	3.75	6.00
10.00	5.00	5.83	10	8.33	4.17	6.67
11.00	5.50	6.42	11	9.17	4.58	7.33
			DAYS.			
03	02	02	1	03	01	02
07	03	04	2	06	03	04
10	05	06	3	08	04	07
13	07	08	4	11	06	09
17	08	10	**5**	14	07	11
20	10	12	6	17	08	13
23	12	14	7	19	10	16
27	13	16	8	22	11	18
30	15	18	9	25	13	20
33	17	19	**10**	28	14	22
37	18	21	11	31	15	24
40	20	23	12	33	17	27
43	22	25	13	36	18	29
47	23	27	14	39	19	31
50	25	29	**15**	42	21	33
53	27	31	16	44	22	36
57	28	33	17	47	24	38
60	30	35	18	50	25	40
63	32	37	19	53	26	42
67	33	39	**20**	56	28	44
70	35	41	21	58	29	47
73	37	43	22	61	31	49
77	38	45	23	64	32	51
80	40	47	24	67	33	53
83	42	49	**25**	69	35	56
87	43	51	26	72	36	58
90	45	53	27	75	38	60
93	47	54	28	78	39	62
97	48	56	29	81	40	64
1.00	50	58	**30**	83	42	67
1.10	55	64	33	92	46	73
2.10	1.05	1.23	63	1.75	88	1.41
3.10	1.55	1.81	93	2.58	1.29	2.07

200 Dollars.

12 PER CENT.	6 PER CENT.	7 PER CENT.	YEARS.	10 PER CENT.	5 PER CENT.	8 PER CENT.
24.00	12.00	14.00	1	20.00	10.00	16.00
48.00	24.00	28.00	2	40.00	20.00	32.00
72.00	36.00	42.00	3	60.00	30.00	48.00
96.00	48.00	56.00	4	80.00	40.00	64.00
120.00	60.00	70.00	5	100.00	50.00	80.00
			MONTHS.			
2.00	1.00	1.17	1	1.67	83	1.33
4.00	2.00	2.33	2	3.33	1.67	2.67
6.00	3.00	3.50	3	5.00	2.50	4.00
8.00	4.00	4.67	4	6.67	3.33	5.33
10.00	5.00	5.83	5	8.33	4.17	6.67
12.00	6.00	7.00	**6**	10.00	5.00	8.00
14.00	7.00	8.17	7	11.67	5.83	9.33
16.00	8.00	9.33	8	13.33	6.67	10.67
18.00	9.00	10.50	9	15.00	7.50	12.00
20.00	10.00	11.67	10	16.67	8.33	13.33
22.00	11.00	12.83	11	18.33	9.17	14.67
			DAYS.			
07	03	04	1	06	03	04
13	07	08	2	11	06	09
20	10	12	3	17	08	13
27	13	16	4	22	11	18
33	17	19	**5**	28	14	22
40	20	23	6	33	17	27
47	23	27	7	39	19	31
53	27	31	8	44	22	36
60	30	35	9	50	25	40
67	33	39	**10**	56	28	44
73	37	43	11	61	31	49
80	40	47	12	67	33	53
87	43	51	13	72	36	58
93	47	54	14	78	39	62
1.00	50	58	**15**	83	42	67
1.07	53	62	16	89	44	71
1.13	57	66	17	94	47	76
1.20	60	70	18	1.00	50	80
1.27	63	74	19	1.06	53	84
1.33	67	78	**20**	1.11	56	89
1.40	70	82	21	1.17	58	93
1.47	73	86	22	1.22	61	98
1.53	77	89	23	1.28	64	1.02
1.60	80	93	24	1.33	67	1.07
1.67	83	97	**25**	1.39	69	1.11
1.73	87	1.01	26	1.44	72	1.16
1.80	90	1.05	27	1.50	75	1.20
1.87	93	1.09	28	1.56	78	1.24
1.93	97	1.13	29	1.61	81	1.29
2.00	1.00	1.17	**30**	1.67	83	1.33
2.20	1.10	1.28	33	1.83	92	1.47
4.20	2.10	2.45	63	3.50	1.75	2.80
6.20	3.10	3.62	93	5.17	2.58	4.13

300 Dollars.

12 PER CENT.	6 PER CENT.	7 PER CENT.	YEARS.	10 PER CENT.	5 PER CENT.	8 PER CENT.
36.00	18.00	21.00	1	30.00	15.00	24.00
72.00	36.00	42.00	2	60.00	30.00	48.00
108.00	54.00	63.00	3	90.00	45.00	72.00
144.00	72.00	84.00	4	120.00	60.00	96.00
180.00	90.00	105.00	5	150.00	75.00	120.00
			MONTHS.			
3.00	1.50	1.75	1	2.50	1.25	2.00
6.00	3.00	3.50	2	5.00	2.50	4.00
9.00	4.50	5.25	3	7.50	3.75	6.00
12.00	6.00	7.00	4	10.00	5.00	8.00
15.00	7.50	8.75	5	12.50	6.25	10.00
18.00	9.00	10.50	**6**	15.00	7.50	12.00
21.00	10.50	12.25	7	17.50	8.75	14.00
24.00	12.00	14.00	8	20.00	10.00	16.00
27.00	13.50	15.75	9	22.50	11.25	18.00
30.00	15.00	17.50	10	25.00	12.50	20.00
33.00	16.50	19.25	11	27.50	13.75	22.00
			DAYS.			
10	05	06	1	08	04	07
20	10	12	2	17	08	13
30	15	18	3	25	13	20
40	20	23	4	33	17	27
50	25	29	**5**	42	21	33
60	30	35	6	50	25	40
70	35	41	7	58	29	47
80	40	47	8	67	33	53
90	45	53	9	75	38	60
1.00	50	58	**10**	83	42	67
1.10	55	64	11	92	46	73
1.20	60	70	12	1.00	50	80
1.30	65	76	13	1.08	54	87
1.40	70	82	14	1.17	58	93
1.50	75	88	**15**	1.25	63	1.00
1.60	80	93	16	1.33	67	1.07
1.70	85	99	17	1.42	71	1.13
1.80	90	1.05	18	1.50	75	1.20
1.90	95	1.11	19	1.58	79	1.27
2.00	1.00	1.17	**20**	1.67	83	1.33
2.10	1.05	1.23	21	1.75	88	1.40
2.20	1.10	1.28	22	1.83	92	1.47
2.30	1.15	1.34	23	1.92	96	1.53
2.40	1.20	1.40	24	2.00	1.00	1.60
2.50	1.25	1.46	**25**	2.08	1.04	1.67
2 60	1.30	1.52	26	2.17	1.08	1.73
2.70	1.35	1.58	27	2.25	1.13	1.80
2.80	1.40	1.63	28	2.33	1.17	1.87
2.90	1.45	1.69	29	2.42	1.21	1.93
3.00	1.50	1.75	**30**	2.50	1.25	2.00
3.30	1.65	1.93	33	2.75	1.38	2.20
6.30	3.15	3.68	63	5.25	2.63	4.20
9.30	4.65	5.43	93	7.75	3.88	6.20

400 Dollars.

12 PER CENT.	6 PER CENT.	7 PER CENT.	YEARS.	10 PER CENT.	5 PER CENT.	8 PER CENT.
48.00	24.00	28.00	1	40.00	20.00	32.00
96.00	48.00	56.00	2	80.00	40.00	64.00
144.00	72.00	84.00	3	120.00	60.00	96.00
192.00	96.00	112.00	4	160.00	80.00	128.00
240.00	120.00	140.00	5	200.00	100.00	160.00
			MONTHS.			
4.00	2.00	2.33	1	3.33	1.67	2.67
8.00	4.00	4.67	2	6.67	3.33	5.33
12.00	6.00	7.00	3	10.00	5.00	8.00
16.00	8.00	9.33	4	13.33	6.67	10.67
20.00	10.00	11.67	5	16.67	8.33	13.33
24.00	12.00	14.00	**6**	20.00	10.00	16.00
28.00	14.00	16.33	7	23.33	11.67	18.67
32.00	16.00	18.67	8	26.67	13.33	21.33
36.00	18.00	21.00	9	30.00	15.00	24.00
40.00	20.00	23.33	10	33.33	16.67	26.67
44.00	22.00	25.67	11	36.67	18.33	29.33
			DAYS.			
13	07	08	1	11	06	09
27	13	16	2	22	11	18
40	20	23	3	33	17	27
53	27	31	4	44	22	36
67	33	39	**5**	56	28	44
80	40	47	6	67	33	53
93	47	54	7	78	39	62
1.07	53	62	8	89	44	71
1.20	60	70	9	1.00	50	80
1.33	67	78	**10**	1.11	56	89
1.47	73	86	11	1.22	61	98
1.60	80	93	12	1.33	67	1.07
1.73	87	1.01	13	1.44	72	1.16
1.87	93	1.09	14	1.56	78	1.24
2.00	1.00	1.17	**15**	1.67	83	1.33
2.13	1.07	1.24	16	1.78	89	1.42
2.27	1.13	1.32	17	1.89	94	1.51
2.40	1.20	1.40	18	2.00	1.00	1.60
2.53	1.27	1.48	19	2.11	1.06	1.69
2.67	1.33	1.56	**20**	2.22	1.11	1.78
2.80	1.40	1.63	21	2.33	1.17	1.87
2.93	1.47	1.71	22	2.44	1.22	1.96
3.07	1.53	1.79	23	2.56	1.28	2.04
3.20	1.60	1.87	24	2.67	1.33	2.13
3.33	1.67	1.94	**25**	2.78	1.39	2.22
3.47	1.73	2.02	26	2.89	1.44	2.31
3.60	1.80	2.10	27	3.00	1.50	2.40
3.73	1.87	2.18	28	3.11	1.56	2.49
3.87	1.93	2.26	29	3.22	1.61	2.58
4.00	2.00	2.33	**30**	3.33	1.67	2.67
4.40	2.20	2.57	33	3.67	1.83	2.94
8.40	4.20	4.90	63	7.00	3.50	5.61
12.40	6.20	7.23	93	10.33	5.17	8.27

500 Dollars.

12 PER CENT.	6 PER CENT.	7 PER CENT.	YEARS.	10 PER CENT.	5 PER CENT.	8 PER CENT.
60.00	30.00	35.00	1	50.00	25.00	40.00
120.00	60.00	70.00	2	100.00	50.00	80.00
180.00	90.00	105.00	3	150.00	75.00	120.00
240.00	120.00	140.00	4	200.00	100.00	160.00
300.00	150.00	175.00	5	250.00	125.00	200.00
			MONTHS.			
5.00	2.50	2.92	1	4.17	2.08	3.33
10.00	5.00	5.83	2	8.33	4.17	6.67
15.00	7.50	8.75	3	12.50	6.25	10.00
20.00	10.00	11.67	4	16.67	8.33	13.33
25.00	12.50	14.58	5	20.83	10.42	16.67
30.00	15.00	17.50	**6**	25.00	12.50	20.00
35.00	17.50	20.42	7	29.17	14.58	23.33
40.00	20.00	23.33	8	33.33	16.67	26.67
45.00	22.50	26.25	9	37.50	18.75	30.00
50.00	25.00	29.17	10	41.67	20.83	33.33
55.00	27.50	32.08	11	45.83	22.92	36.67
			DAYS.			
17	08	10	1	14	07	11
33	17	19	2	28	14	22
50	25	29	3	42	21	33
67	33	39	4	56	28	44
83	42	49	**5**	69	35	56
1.00	50	58	6	83	42	67
1.17	58	68	7	97	49	78
1.33	67	78	8	1.11	56	89
1.50	75	88	9	1.25	63	1.00
1.67	83	97	**10**	1.39	69	1.11
1.83	92	1.07	11	1.53	76	1.22
2.00	1.00	1.17	12	1.67	83	1.33
2.17	1.08	1.26	13	1.81	90	1.44
2.33	1.17	1.36	14	1.94	97	1.56
2.50	1.25	1.46	**15**	2.08	1.04	1.67
2.67	1.33	1.56	16	2.22	1.11	1.78
2.83	1.42	1.65	17	2.36	1.18	1.89
3.00	1.50	1.75	18	2.50	1.25	2.00
3.17	1.58	1.85	19	2.64	1.32	2.11
3.33	1.67	1.94	**20**	2.78	1.39	2.22
3.50	1.75	2.04	21	2.92	1.46	2.33
3.67	1.83	2.14	22	3.06	1.53	2.44
3.83	1.92	2.24	23	3.19	1.60	2.56
4.00	2.00	2.33	24	3.33	1.67	2.67
4.17	2.08	2.43	**25**	3.47	1.74	2.78
4.33	2.17	2.53	26	3.61	1.81	2.89
4.50	2.25	2.63	27	3.75	1.88	3.00
4.67	2.33	2.72	28	3.89	1.94	3.11
4.83	2.42	2.82	29	4.03	2.01	3.22
5.00	2.50	2.92	**30**	4.17	2.08	3.33
5.50	2.75	3.21	33	4.58	2.29	3.66
10.50	5.25	6.13	63	8.75	4.38	7.00
15.50	7.75	9.04	93	12.91	6.46	10.32

600 Dollars.

12 PER CENT.	6 PER CENT.	7 PER CENT.	YEARS.	10 PER CENT.	5 PER CENT.	8 PER CENT.
72.00	36.00	42.00	1	60.00	30.00	48.00
144.00	72.00	84.00	2	120.00	60.00	96.00
216.00	108.00	126.00	3	180.00	90.00	144.00
288.00	144.00	168.00	4	240.00	120.00	192.00
360.00	180.00	210.00	5	300.00	150.00	240.00
			MONTHS.			
6.00	3.00	3.50	1	5.00	2.50	4.00
12.00	6.00	7.00	2	10.00	5.00	8.00
18.00	9.00	10.50	3	15.00	7.50	12.00
24.00	12.00	14.00	4	20.00	10.00	16.00
30.00	15.00	17.50	5	25.00	12.50	20.00
36.00	18.00	21.00	**6**	30.00	15.00	24.00
42.00	21.00	24.50	7	35.00	17.50	28.00
48.00	24.00	28.00	8	40.00	20.00	32.00
54.00	27.00	31.50	9	45.00	22.50	36.00
60.00	30.00	35.00	10	50.00	25.00	40.00
66.00	33.00	38.50	11	55.00	27.50	44.00
			DAYS.			
20	10	12	1	17	08	13
40	20	23	2	33	17	27
60	30	35	3	50	25	40
80	40	47	4	67	33	53
1.00	50	58	**5**	83	42	67
1.20	60	70	6	1.00	50	80
1.40	70	82	7	1.17	58	93
1.60	80	93	8	1.33	67	1.07
1.80	90	1.05	9	1.50	75	1.20
2.00	1.00	1.17	**10**	1.67	83	1.33
2.20	1.10	1.28	11	1.83	92	1.47
2.40	1.20	1.40	12	2.00	1.00	1.60
2.60	1.30	1.52	13	2.17	1.08	1.73
2.80	1.40	1.63	14	2.33	1.17	1.87
3.00	1.50	1.75	**15**	2.50	1.25	2.00
3.20	1.60	1.87	16	2.67	1.33	2.13
3.40	1.70	1.98	17	2.83	1.42	2.27
3.60	1.80	2.10	18	3.00	1.50	2.40
3.80	1.90	2.22	19	3.17	1.58	2.53
4.00	2.00	2.33	**20**	3.33	1.67	2.67
4.20	2.10	2.45	21	3.50	1.75	2.80
4.40	2.20	2.57	22	3.67	1.83	2.93
4.60	2.30	2.68	23	3.83	1.92	3.07
4.80	2.40	2.80	24	4.00	2.00	3.20
5.00	2.50	2.92	**25**	4.17	2.08	3.33
5.20	2.60	3.03	26	4.33	2.17	3.47
5.40	2.70	3.15	27	4.50	2.25	3.60
5.60	2.80	3.27	28	4.67	2.33	3.73
5.80	2.90	3.38	29	4.83	2.42	3.87
6.00	3.00	3.50	**30**	5.00	2.50	4.00
6.60	3.30	3.85	33	5.50	2.75	4.40
12.60	6.30	7.35	63	10.50	5.25	8.40
18.60	9.30	10.85	93	15.50	7.75	12.40

700 Dollars.

12 PER CENT.	6 PER CENT.	7 PER CENT.	YEARS.	10 PER CENT.	5 PER CENT.	8 PER CENT.
84.00	42.00	49.00	1	70.00	35.00	56.00
168.00	84.00	98.00	2	140.00	70.00	112.00
252.00	126.00	147.00	3	210.00	105.00	168.00
336.00	168.00	196.00	4	280.00	140.00	224.00
420.00	210.00	245.00	5	350.00	175.00	280.00
			MONTHS.			
7.00	3.50	4.08	1	5.83	2.92	4.67
14.00	7.00	8.17	2	11.67	5.83	9.33
21.00	10.50	12.25	3	17.50	8.75	14.00
28.00	14.00	16.33	4	23.33	11.67	18.67
35.00	17.50	20.42	5	29.17	14.58	23.33
42.00	21.00	24.50	**6**	35.00	17.50	28.00
49.00	24.50	28.58	7	40.83	20.42	32.67
56.00	28.00	32.67	8	46.67	23.33	37.33
63.00	31.50	36.75	9	52.50	26.25	42.00
70.00	35.00	40.83	10	58.33	29.17	46.67
77.00	38.50	44.92	11	64.17	32.08	51.33
			DAYS.			
23	12	14	1	19	10	16
47	23	27	2	39	19	31
70	35	41	3	58	29	47
93	47	54	4	78	39	62
1.17	58	68	**5**	97	49	78
1.40	70	82	6	1.17	58	93
1.63	82	95	7	1.36	68	1.09
1.87	93	1.09	8	1.56	78	1.24
2.10	1.05	1.23	9	1.75	88	1.40
2.33	1.17	1.36	**10**	1.94	97	1.56
2.57	1.28	1.50	11	2.14	1.07	1.71
2.80	1.40	1.63	12	2.33	1.17	1.87
3.03	1.52	1.77	13	2.53	1.26	2.02
3.27	1.63	1.91	14	2.72	1.36	2.18
3.50	1.75	2.04	**15**	2.92	1.46	2.33
3.73	1.87	2.18	16	3.11	1.56	2.49
3.97	1.98	2.31	17	3.31	1.65	2.64
4.20	2.10	2.45	18	3.50	1.75	2.80
4.43	2.22	2.59	19	3.69	1.85	2.96
4.67	2.33	2.72	**20**	3.89	1.94	3.11
4.90	2.45	2.86	21	4.08	2.04	3.27
5.13	2.57	2.99	22	4.28	2.14	3.42
5.37	2.68	3.13	23	4.47	2.24	3.58
5.60	2.80	3.27	24	4.67	2.33	3.73
5.83	2.92	3.40	**25**	4.86	2.43	3.89
6.07	3.03	3.54	26	5.06	2.53	4.04
6.30	3.15	3.68	27	5.25	2.63	4.20
6.53	3.27	3.81	28	5.44	2.72	4.36
6.77	3.38	3.95	29	5.64	2.82	4.51
7.00	3.50	4.08	**30**	5.83	2.92	4.67
7.70	3.85	4.49	33	6.42	3.21	5.13
14.70	7.35	8.57	63	12.25	6.13	9.80
21.70	10.85	12.66	93	18.08	9.04	14.47

800 Dollars.

12 PER CENT.	6 PER CENT.	7 PER CENT.	YEARS.	10 PER CENT.	5 PER CENT.	8 PER CENT.
96.00	48.00	56.00	1	80.00	40.00	64.00
192.00	96.00	112.00	2	160.00	80.00	128.00
288.00	144.00	168.00	3	240.00	120.00	192.00
384.00	192.00	224.00	4	320.00	160.00	256.00
480.00	240.00	280.00	5	400.00	200.00	320.00
			MONTHS.			
8.00	4.00	4.67	1	6.67	3.33	5.33
16.00	8.00	9.33	2	13.33	6.67	10.67
24.00	12.00	14.00	3	20.00	10.00	16.00
32.00	16.00	18.67	4	26.67	13.33	21.33
40.00	20.00	23.33	5	33.33	16.67	26.67
48.00	24.00	28.00	**6**	40.00	20.00	32.00
56.00	28.00	32.67	7	46.67	23.33	37.33
64.00	32.00	37.33	8	53.33	26.67	42.67
72.00	36.00	42.00	9	60.00	30.00	48.00
80.00	40.00	46.67	10	66.67	33.33	53.33
88.00	44.00	51.33	11	73.33	36.67	58.67
			DAYS.			
27	13	16	1	22	11	18
53	27	31	2	44	22	36
80	40	47	3	67	33	53
1.07	53	62	4	89	44	71
1.33	67	78	**5**	1.11	56	89
1.60	80	93	6	1.33	67	1.07
1.87	93	1.09	7	1.56	78	1.24
2.13	1.07	1.24	8	1.78	89	1.42
2.40	1.20	1.40	9	2.00	1.00	1.60
2.66	1.33	1.56	**10**	2.22	1.11	1.78
2.93	1.47	1.71	11	2.44	1.22	1.96
3.20	1.60	1.87	12	2.67	1.33	2.13
3.47	1.73	2.02	13	2.89	1.44	2.31
3.73	1.87	2.18	14	3.11	1.56	2.49
4.00	2.00	2.33	**15**	3.33	1.67	2.67
4.27	2.13	2.49	16	3.56	1.78	2.84
4.53	2.27	2.64	17	3.78	1.89	3.02
4.80	2.40	2.80	18	4.00	2.00	3.20
5.07	2.53	2.96	19	4.22	2.11	3.38
5.33	2.67	3.11	**20**	4.44	2.22	3.56
5.60	2.80	3.27	21	4.67	2.33	3.73
5.87	2.93	3.42	22	4.89	2.44	3.91
6.13	3.07	3.58	23	5.11	2.56	4.09
6.40	3 20	3.73	24	5.33	2.67	4.27
6.67	3.33	3.89	**25**	5.56	2.78	4.44
6.93	3.47	4.04	26	5.78	2.89	4.62
7.20	3.60	4.20	27	6.00	3.00	4.80
7.47	3.73	4.36	28	6.22	3.11	4.98
7.73	3.87	4.51	29	6.44	3.22	5.16
8.00	4.00	4.67	**30**	6.67	3.33	5.33
8.80	4.40	5.13	33	7.33	3.67	5.87
16.80	8.40	9.80	63	14.00	7.00	11.20
24.80	12.40	14.47	93	20.67	10.33	16.53

900 Dollars.

12 PER CENT.	6 PER CENT.	7 PER CENT.	YEARS.	10 PER CENT.	5 PER CENT.	8 PER CENT.
108.00	54.00	63.00	1	90.00	45.00	72.00
216.00	108.00	126.00	2	180.00	90.00	144.00
324.00	162.00	189.00	3	270.00	135.00	216.00
432.00	216.00	252.00	4	360.00	180.00	288.00
540.00	270.00	315.00	5	450.00	225.00	360.00
			MONTHS.			
9.00	4.50	5.25	1	7.50	3.75	6.00
18.00	9.00	10.50	2	15.00	7.50	12.00
27.00	13.50	15.75	3	22.50	11.25	18.00
36.00	18.00	21.00	4	30.00	15.00	24.00
45.00	22.50	26.25	5	37.50	18.75	30.00
54.00	27.00	31.50	**6**	45.00	22.50	36.00
63.00	31.50	36.75	7	52.50	26.25	42.00
72.00	36.00	42.00	8	60.00	30.00	48.00
81.00	40.50	47.25	9	67.50	33.75	54.00
90.00	45.00	52.50	10	75.00	37.50	60.00
99.00	49.50	57.75	11	82.50	41.25	66.00
			DAYS.			
30	15	18	1	25	13	20
60	30	35	2	50	25	40
90	45	53	3	75	38	60
1.20	60	70	4	1.00	50	80
1.50	75	88	**5**	1.25	63	1.00
1.80	90	1.05	6	1.50	75	1.20
2.10	1.05	1.23	7	1.75	88	1.40
2.40	1.20	1.40	8	2.00	1.00	1.60
2.70	1.35	1.58	9	2.25	1.13	1.80
3.00	1.50	1.75	**10**	2.50	1.25	2.00
3.30	1.65	1.93	11	2.75	1.38	2.20
3.60	1.80	2.10	12	3.00	1.50	2.40
3.90	1.95	2.28	13	3.25	1.63	2.60
4.20	2.10	2.45	14	3.50	1.75	2.80
4.50	2.25	2.63	**15**	3.75	1.88	3.00
4.80	2.40	2.80	16	4.00	2.00	3.20
5.10	2.55	2.98	17	4.25	2.13	3.40
5.40	2.70	3.15	18	4.50	2.25	3.60
5.70	2.85	3.33	19	4.75	2.38	3.80
6.00	3.00	3.50	**20**	5.00	2.50	4.00
6.30	3.15	3.68	21	5.25	2.63	4.20
6.60	3.30	3.85	22	5.50	2.75	4.40
6.90	3.45	4.03	23	5.75	2.88	4.60
7.20	3.60	4.20	24	6.00	3.00	4.80
7.50	3.75	4.38	**25**	6.25	3.13	5.00
7.80	3.90	4.55	26	6.50	3.25	5.20
8.10	4.05	4.73	27	6.75	3.38	5.40
8.40	4.20	4.90	28	7.00	3.50	5.60
8.70	4.35	5.08	29	7.25	3.63	5.80
9.00	4.50	5.25	**30**	7.50	3.75	6.00
9.90	4.95	5.78	33	8.25	4.13	6.60
18.90	9.45	11.03	63	15.75	7.[illegible]8	12.60
27.90	13.95	16.28	93	23.25	11.63	18.60

1,000 Dollars.

12 PER CENT.	6 PER CENT.	7 PER CENT.	YEARS.	10 PER CENT.	5 PER CENT.	8 PER CENT.
120.00	60.00	70.00	1	100.00	50.00	80.00
240.00	120.00	140.00	2	200.00	100.00	160.00
360.00	180.00	210.00	3	300.00	150.00	240.00
480.00	240.00	280.00	4	400.00	200.00	320.00
600.00	300.00	350.00	5	500.00	250.00	400.00
			MONTHS.			
10.00	5.00	5.83	1	8.33	4.17	6.67
20.00	10.00	11.67	2	16.67	8.33	13.33
30.00	15.00	17.50	3	25.00	12.50	20.00
40.00	20.00	23.33	4	33.33	16.67	26.67
50.00	25.00	29.17	5	41.67	20.83	33.33
60.00	30.00	35.00	**6**	50.00	25.00	40.00
70.00	35.00	40.83	7	58.33	29.17	46.67
80.00	40.00	46.67	8	66.67	33.33	53.33
90.00	45.00	52.50	9	75.00	37.50	60.00
100.00	50.00	58.33	10	83.33	41.67	66.67
110.00	55.00	64.17	11	91.67	45.83	73.33
			DAYS.			
33	17	19	1	28	14	22
67	33	39	2	56	28	44
1.00	50	58	3	83	42	67
1.33	67	78	4	1.11	56	89
1.67	83	97	**5**	1.39	69	1.11
2.00	1.00	1.17	6	1.67	83	1.33
2.33	1.17	1.36	7	1.94	97	1.56
2.67	1.33	1.56	8	2.22	1.11	1.78
3.00	1.50	1.75	9	2.50	1.25	2.00
3.33	1.67	1.94	**10**	2.78	1.39	2.22
3.67	1.83	2.14	11	3.06	1.53	2.44
4.00	2.00	2.33	12	3.33	1.67	2.67
4.33	2.17	2.53	13	3.61	1.81	2.89
4.67	2.33	2.72	14	3.89	1.94	3.11
5.00	2.50	2.92	**15**	4.17	2.08	3.33
5.33	2.67	3.11	16	4.44	2.22	3.56
5.67	2.83	3.31	17	4.72	2.36	3.78
6.00	3.00	3.50	18	5.00	2.50	4.00
6.33	3.17	3.69	19	5.28	2.64	4.22
6.67	3.33	3.89	**20**	5.56	2.78	4.44
7.00	3.50	4.08	21	5.83	2.92	4.67
7.33	3.67	4.28	22	6.11	3.06	4.89
7.67	3.83	4.47	23	6.39	3.19	5.11
8.00	4.00	4.67	24	6.67	3.33	5.33
8.33	4.17	4.86	**25**	6.94	3.47	5.56
8.67	4.33	5.06	26	7.22	3.61	5.78
9.00	4.50	5.25	27	7.50	3.75	6.00
9.33	4.67	5.44	28	7.78	3.89	6.22
9.67	4.83	5.64	29	8.06	4.03	6.44
10.00	5.00	5.83	**30**	8.33	4.17	6.67
11.00	5.50	6.42	33	9.17	4.58	7.34
21.00	10.50	12.25	63	17.50	8.75	14.01
31.00	15.50	18.08	93	25.83	12.92	20.68

2,000 Dollars.

12 PER CENT.	6 PER CENT.	7 PER CENT.	YEARS.	10 PER CENT.	5 PER CENT.	8 PER CENT.
240.00	120.00	140.00	1	200.00	100.00	160.00
480.00	240.00	280.00	2	400.00	200.00	320.00
720.00	360.00	420.00	3	600.00	300.00	480.00
960.00	480.00	560.00	4	800.00	400.00	640.00
1200.00	600.00	700.00	5	1000.00	500.00	800.00
			MONTHS.			
20.00	10.00	11.67	1	16.67	8.33	13.33
40.00	20.00	23.33	2	33.33	16.67	26.67
60.00	30.00	35.00	3	50.00	25.00	40.00
80.00	40.00	46.67	4	66.67	33.33	53.33
100.00	50.00	58.33	5	83.33	41.67	66.67
120.00	60.00	70.00	**6**	100.00	50.00	80.00
140.00	70.00	81.67	7	116.67	58.33	93.33
160.00	80.00	93.33	8	133.33	66.67	106.67
180.00	90.00	105.00	9	150.00	75.00	120.00
200.00	100.00	116.67	10	166.67	83.33	133.33
220.00	110.00	128.33	11	183.33	91.67	146.67
			DAYS.			
67	33	39	1	56	28	44
1.33	67	78	2	1.11	56	89
2.00	1.00	1.17	3	1.67	83	1.33
2.67	1.33	1.56	4	2.22	1.11	1.78
3.33	1.67	1.94	**5**	2.78	1.39	2.22
4.00	2.00	2.33	6	3.33	1.67	2.67
4.67	2.33	2.72	7	3.89	1.94	3.11
5.33	2.67	3.11	8	4.44	2.22	3.56
6.00	3.00	3.50	9	5.00	2.50	4.00
6.67	3.33	3.89	**10**	5.56	2.78	4.44
7.33	3.67	4.28	11	6.11	3.06	4.89
8.00	4.00	4.67	12	6.67	3.33	5.33
8.67	4.33	5.06	13	7.22	3.61	5.78
9.33	4.67	5.44	14	7.78	3.89	6.22
10.00	5.00	5.83	**15**	8.33	4.17	6.67
10.67	5.33	6.22	16	8.89	4.44	7.11
11.33	5.67	6.61	17	9.44	4.72	7.56
12.00	6.00	7.00	18	10.00	5.00	8.00
12.67	6.33	7.39	19	10.56	5.28	8.44
13.33	6.67	7.78	**20**	11.11	5.56	8.89
14.00	7.00	8.17	21	11.67	5.83	9.33
14.67	7.33	8.56	22	12.22	6.11	9.78
15.33	7.67	8.94	23	12.78	6.39	10.22
16.00	8.00	9.33	24	13.33	6.67	10.67
16.67	8.33	9.72	**25**	13.89	6.94	11.11
17.33	8.67	10.11	26	14.44	7.22	11.56
18.00	9.00	10.50	27	15.00	7.50	12.00
18.67	9.33	10.89	28	15.56	7.78	12.44
19.33	9.67	11.28	29	16.11	8.06	12.89
20.00	10.00	11.67	**30**	16.67	8.33	13.33
22.00	11.00	12.83	33	18.34	9.17	14.66
42.00	21.00	24.50	63	35.01	17.50	27.99
62.00	31.00	36.17	93	51.68	25.83	41.32

3,000 Dollars.

12 PER CENT.	6 PER CENT.	7 PER CENT.		10 PER CENT.	5 PER CENT.	8 PER CENT.
			YEARS.			
360.00	180.00	210.00	1	300.00	150.00	240.00
720.00	360.00	420.00	2	600.00	300.00	480.00
1080.00	540.00	630.00	3	900.00	450.00	720.00
1440.00	720.00	840.00	4	1200.00	600.00	960.00
1800.00	900.00	1050.00	5	1500.00	750.00	1200.00
			MONTHS.			
30.00	15.00	17.50	1	25.00	12.50	20.00
60.00	30.00	35.00	2	50.00	25.00	40.00
90.00	45.00	52.50	3	75 00	37.50	60.00
120.00	60.00	70.00	4	100.00	50.00	80.00
150.00	75.00	87.50	5	125.00	62.50	100.00
180.00	90.00	105.00	**6**	150.00	75.00	120.00
210.00	105.00	122.50	7	175.00	87.50	140.00
240.00	120.00	140.00	8	200.00	100.00	160.00
270.00	135.00	157.50	9	225.00	112.50	180.00
300.00	150.00	175.00	10	250.00	125.00	200.00
330.00	165.00	192.50	11	275.00	137.50	220.00
			DAYS.			
1.00	50	58	1	83	42	67
2.00	1.00	1.17	2	1.67	83	1.33
3.00	1.50	1.75	3	2.50	1.25	2.00
4.00	2.00	2.33	4	3.33	1.67	2.67
5.00	2.50	2.92	**5**	4.17	2.08	3.33
6.00	3.00	3.50	6	5.00	2.50	4.00
7.00	3.50	4.08	7	5.83	2.92	4.67
8.00	4.00	4.67	8	6.67	3.33	5.33
9.00	4.50	5.25	9	7.50	3.75	6.00
10.00	5.00	5.83	**10**	8.33	4.17	6.67
11.00	5.50	6.42	11	9.17	4.58	7.33
12.00	6.00	7.00	12	10.00	5.00	8.00
13.00	6.50	7.58	13	10.83	5.42	8.67
14.00	7.00	8.17	14	11.67	5.83	9.33
15.00	7.50	8.75	**15**	12.50	6.25	10.00
16.00	8.00	9.33	16	13.33	6.67	10.67
17.00	8.50	9.92	17	14.17	7.08	11.33
18.00	9.00	10.50	18	15.00	7.50	12.00
19.00	9.50	11.08	19	15.83	7.92	12.67
20.00	10.00	11.67	**20**	16.67	8.33	13.33
21.00	10.50	12.25	21	17.50	8.75	14.00
22.00	11.00	12.83	22	18.33	9.17	14.67
23.00	11.50	13.42	23	19.17	9.58	15.33
24.00	12.00	14.00	24	20.00	10.00	16.00
25.00	12.50	14.58	**25**	20.83	10.42	16.67
26.00	13.00	15.17	26	21.67	10.83	17.33
27.00	13.50	15.75	27	22.50	11.25	18.00
28.00	14.00	16.33	28	23.33	11.67	18.67
29.00	14.50	16.92	29	24.17	12.08	19.33
30.00	15.00	17.50	**30**	25.00	12.50	20.00
33.00	16.50	19.25	33	27.50	13.75	22.00
63.00	31.50	36.75	63	52.50	26.25	42.00
93.00	46.50	54.25	93	77.50	38.75	62 00

4,000 Dollars.

12 PER CENT.	6 PER CENT.	7 PER CENT.	YEARS.	10 PER CENT.	5 PER CENT.	8 PER CENT.
480.00	240.00	280.00	1	400.00	200.00	320.00
960.00	480.00	560.00	2	800.00	400.00	640.00
1440.00	720.00	840.00	3	1200.00	600.00	960.00
1920.00	960.00	1120.00	4	1600.00	800.00	1280.00
2400.00	1200.00	1400.00	5	2000.00	1000.00	1600.00
			MONTHS.			
40.00	20.00	23.33	1	33.33	16.67	26.67
80.00	40.00	46.67	2	66.67	33.33	53.33
120.00	60.00	70.00	3	100.00	50.00	80.00
160.00	80.00	93.33	4	133.33	66.67	106.67
200.00	100.00	116.67	5	166.67	83.33	133.33
240.00	120.00	140.00	**6**	200.00	100.00	160.00
280.00	140.00	163.33	7	233.33	116.67	186.67
320.00	160.00	186.67	8	266.67	133.33	213.33
360.00	180.00	210.00	9	300.00	150.00	240.00
400.00	200.00	233.33	10	333.33	166.67	266.67
440.00	220.00	256.67	11	366.67	183.33	293.33
			DAYS.			
1.33	67	78	1	1.11	56	89
2.67	1.33	1.56	2	2.22	1.11	1.78
4.00	2.00	2.33	3	3.33	1.67	2.67
5.33	2.67	3.11	4	4.44	2.22	3.56
6.67	3.33	3.89	**5**	5.56	2.78	4.44
8.00	4.00	4.67	6	6.67	3.33	5.33
9.33	4.67	5.44	7	7.78	3.89	6.22
10.67	5.33	6.22	8	8.89	4.44	7.11
12.00	6.00	7.00	9	10.00	5.00	8.00
13.33	6.67	7.78	**10**	11.11	5.56	8.89
14.67	7.33	8.56	11	12.22	6.11	9.78
16.00	8.00	9.33	12	13.33	6.67	10.67
17.33	8.67	10.11	13	14.44	7.22	11.56
18.67	9.33	10.89	14	15.56	7.78	12.44
20.00	10.00	11.67	**15**	16.67	8.33	13.33
21.33	10·67	12.44	16	17.78	8.89	14.22
22.67	11.33	13.22	17	18.89	9.44	15.11
24.00	12.00	14.00	18	20.00	10.00	16.00
25.33	12.67	14.78	19	21.11	10.56	16.89
26.67	13.33	15.56	**20**	22.22	11.11	17.78
28.00	14.00	16.33	21	23.33	11.67	18.67
29.33	14.67	17.11	22	24.44	12.22	19.56
30.67	15.33	17.89	23	25.56	12.78	20.44
32.00	16.00	18.67	24	26.67	13.33	21.33
33.33	16.67	19.44	**25**	27.78	13.89	22.22
34.67	17.33	20.22	26	28.89	14.44	23.11
36.00	18.00	21.00	27	30.00	15.00	24.00
37.33	18.67	21.78	28	31.11	15.56	24.89
38.67	19.33	22.56	29	32.22	16.11	25.78
40.00	20.00	23.33	**30**	33.33	16.67	26.67
44.00	22.00	25.67	33	36.67	18.33	29.33
84.00	42.00	49.00	63	70.00	35.00	56.00
124.00	62.00	72.33	93	103.33	51.67	82.67

5,000 Dollars.

12 PER CENT.	6 PER CENT.	7 PER CENT.	YEARS.	10 PER CENT.	5 PER CENT.	8 PER CENT.
600.00	300.00	350.00	1	500.00	250.00	400.00
1200.00	600.00	700.00	2	1000.00	500.00	800.00
1800.00	900.00	1050.00	3	1500.00	750.00	1200.00
2400.00	1200.00	1400.00	4	2000.00	1000.00	1600.00
3000.00	1500.00	1750.00	5	2500.00	1250.00	2000.00
			MONTHS.			
50.00	25.00	29.17	1	41.67	20.83	33.33
100.00	50.00	58.33	2	83.33	41.67	66.67
150.00	75 00	87.50	3	125.00	62.50	100.00
200.00	100.00	116.67	4	166.67	83.33	133.33
250.00	125.00	145.83	5	208.33	104.17	166.67
300.00	150.00	175.00	**6**	250.00	125.00	200.00
350.00	175.00	204.17	7	291.67	145.83	233.33
400.00	200.00	233.33	8	333.33	166.67	266.67
450.00	225.00	262.50	9	375.00	187.50	300.00
500.00	250.00	291.67	10	416.67	208.33	333.33
550.00	275.00	320.83	11	458.33	229.17	366.67
			DAYS.			
1.67	83	97	1	1.39	69	1.11
3.33	1.67	1.94	2	2.78	1.39	2.22
5.00	2.50	2.92	3	4.17	2.08	3.33
6.67	3.33	3.89	4	5.56	2.78	4.44
8.33	4.17	4.86	**5**	6.94	3.47	5.56
10.00	5.00	5.83	6	8.33	4.17	6.67
11.67	5.83	6.81	7	9.72	4.86	7.78
13.33	6.67	7.78	8	11.11	5.56	8.89
15.00	7.50	8.75	9	12.50	6.25	10.00
16.67	8.33	9.72	**10**	13.89	6.94	11.11
18.33	9.17	10.69	11	15.28	7.64	12.22
20.00	10.00	11.67	12	16.67	8.33	13.33
21.67	10.83	12.64	13	18.06	9.03	14.44
23.33	11.67	13.61	14	19.44	9.72	15.56
25.00	12.50	14.58	**15**	20.83	10.42	16.67
26.67	13:33	15.56	16	22.22	11.11	17.78
28.33	14.17	16.53	17	23.61	11.81	18.89
30.00	15.00	17.50	18	25.00	12.50	20.00
31.67	15.83	18.47	19	26.39	13.19	21.11
33.33	16.67	19.44	**20**	27.78	13.89	22.22
35.00	17.50	20.42	21	29.17	14.58	23.33
36.67	18.33	21.39	22	30.56	15.28	24.44
38.33	19.17	22.36	23	31.94	15.97	25.56
40.00	20.00	23.33	24	33.33	16.67	26.67
41.67	20.83	24.31	**25**	34.72	17.36	27.78
43.33	21.67	25.28	26	36.11	18.06	28.89
45.00	22.50	26.25	27	37.50	18.75	30.00
46.67	23.33	27.22	28	38.89	19.44	31.11
48.33	24.17	28 19	29	40.28	20.14	32.22
50.00	25.00	29.17	**30**	41.67	20.83	33.33
55.00	27.50	32.08	33	45.83	22.92	36.67
105.00	52.50	61.25	63	87.50	43.75	70.00
155.00	77.50	90.41	93	129.17	64.58	103.33

6,000 Dollars.

12 PER CENT.	6 PER CENT.	7 PER CENT.	YEARS.	10 PER CENT.	5 PER CENT.	8 PER CENT.
720.00	360.00	420.00	1	600.00	300.00	480.00
1440.00	720.00	840.00	2	1200.00	600.00	960.00
2160.00	1080.00	1260.00	3	1800.00	900.00	1440.00
2880.00	1440.00	1680.00	4	2400.00	1200.00	1920.00
3600.00	1800.00	2100.00	5	3000.00	1500.00	2400.00
			MONTHS.			
60.00	30.00	35.00	1	50.00	25.00	40.00
120.00	60.00	70.00	2	100.00	50.00	80.00
180.00	90.00	105.00	3	150.00	75.00	120.00
240.00	120.00	140.00	4	200.00	100.00	160.00
300.00	150.00	175.00	5	250.00	125.00	200.00
360.00	180.00	210.00	**6**	300.00	150.00	240.00
420.00	210.00	245.00	7	350.00	175.00	280.00
480.00	240.00	280.00	8	400.00	200.00	320.00
540.00	270.00	315.00	9	450.00	225.00	360.00
600.00	300.00	350.00	10	500.00	250.00	400.00
660.00	330.00	385.00	11	550.00	275.00	440.00
			DAYS.			
2.00	1.00	1.17	1	1.67	83	1.33
4.00	2.00	2.33	2	3.33	1.67	2.67
6.00	3.00	3.50	3	5.00	2.50	4.00
8.00	4.00	4.67	4	6.67	3.33	5.33
10.00	5.00	5.83	**5**	8.33	4.17	6.67
12.00	6.00	7.00	6	10.00	5.00	8.00
14.00	7.00	8.17	7	11.67	5.83	9.33
16.00	8.00	9.33	8	13.33	6.67	10.67
18.00	9.00	10.50	9	15.00	7.50	12.00
20.00	10.00	11.67	**10**	16.67	8.33	13.33
22.00	11.00	12.83	11	18.33	9.17	14.67
24.00	12.00	14.00	12	20.00	10.00	16.00
26.00	13.00	15.17	13	21.67	10.83	17.33
28.00	14.00	16.33	14	23.33	11.67	18.67
30.00	15.00	17.50	**15**	25.00	12.50	20.00
32.00	16.00	18.67	16	26.67	13.33	21.33
34.00	17.00	19.83	17	28.33	14.17	22.67
36.00	18.00	21.00	18	30.00	15 00	24.00
38.00	19.00	22.17	19	31.67	15.83	25.33
40.00	20.00	23.33	**20**	33.33	16.67	26.67
42.00	21.00	24 50	21	35.00	17.50	28.00
44.00	22.00	25.67	22	36.67	18.33	29.33
46.00	23.00	26.83	23	38.33	19.17	30.67
48.00	24.00	28.00	24	40.00	20.00	32.00
50.00	25.00	29.17	**25**	41.67	20.83	33.33
52.00	26.00	30.33	26	43.33	21.67	34.67
54.00	27.00	31.50	27	45.00	22.50	36.00
56.00	28.00	32.67	28	46.67	23.33	37.33
58.00	29.00	33.83	29	48.33	24.17	38.67
60.00	30.00	35.00	**30**	50.00	25.00	40.00
66.00	33.00	38.50	33	55.00	27.50	44.00
126.00	63.00	73.50	63	105.00	52.50	84.00
186.00	93.00	108.50	93	155.00	77.50	124.00

7,000 Dollars.

12 PER CENT.	6 PER CENT.	7 PER CENT.	YEARS.	10 PER CENT.	5 PER CENT.	8 PER CENT.
840.00	420.00	490.00	1	700.00	350.00	560.00
1680.00	840.00	980.00	2	1400.00	700.00	1120.00
2520.00	1260.00	1470.00	3	2100.00	1050.00	1680.00
3360.00	1680.00	1960.00	4	2800.00	1400.00	2240.00
4200.00	2100.00	2450.00	5	3500.00	1750.00	2800.00
			MONTHS.			
70.00	35.00	40.83	1	58.33	29.17	46.67
140.00	70.00	81.67	2	116.67	58.33	93.33
210.00	105.00	122.50	3	175.00	87.50	140.00
280.00	140.00	163.33	4	233.33	116.67	186.67
350.00	175.00	204.17	5	291.67	145.83	233.33
420.00	210.00	245.00	**6**	350.00	175.00	280.00
490.00	245.00	285.83	7	408.33	204.17	326.67
560.00	280.00	326.67	8	466.67	233.33	373.33
630.00	315.00	367.50	9	525.00	262.50	420.00
700.00	350.00	408.33	10	583.33	291.67	466.67
770.00	385.00	449.17	11	641.67	320.83	513.33
			DAYS.			
2.33	1.17	1.36	1	1.94	97	1.56
4.67	2.33	2.72	2	3.89	1.94	3.11
7.00	3.50	4.08	3	5.83	2.92	4.67
9.33	4.67	5.44	4	7.78	3.89	6.22
11.67	5.83	6.81	**5**	9.72	4.86	7.78
14.00	7.00	8.17	6	11.67	5.83	9.33
16.33	8.17	9.53	7	13.61	6.81	10.89
18.67	9.33	10.89	8	15.56	7.78	12.44
21.00	10.50	12.25	9	17.50	8.75	14.00
23.33	11.67	13.61	**10**	19.44	9.72	15.56
25.67	12.83	14.97	11	21.39	10.69	17.11
28.00	14.00	16.33	12	23.33	11.67	18.67
30.33	15.17	17.69	13	25.28	12.64	20.22
32.67	16.33	19.06	14	27.22	13.61	21.78
35.00	17.50	20.42	**15**	29.17	14.58	23.33
37.33	18.67	21.78	16	31.11	15.56	24.89
39.67	19.83	23.14	17	33.06	16.53	26.44
42.00	21.00	24.50	18	35.00	17.50	28.00
44.33	22.17	25.86	19	36.94	18.47	29.56
46.67	23.33	27.22	**20**	38.89	19.44	31.11
49.00	24.50	28.58	21	40.83	20.42	32.67
51.33	25.67	29.94	22	42.78	21.39	34.22
53.67	26.83	31.31	23	44.72	22.36	35.78
56.00	28.00	32.67	24	46.67	23.33	37.33
58.33	29.17	34.03	**25**	48.61	24.31	38.89
60.67	30.33	35.39	26	50.56	25.28	40.44
63.00	31.50	36.75	27	52.50	26.25	42.00
65.33	32.67	38.11	28	54.44	27.22	43.56
67.67	33.83	39.47	29	56.39	28 19	45.11
70.00	35.00	40.83	**30**	58.33	29.17	46.67
77.00	38.50	44.91	33	64.16	32.08	51.34
147.00	73.50	85.74	63	122.50	61.25	98.00
217.00	108.50	126.58	93	180.83	90.41	144.68

8,000 Dollars.

12 PER CENT.	6 PER CENT.	7 PER CEMT.	YEARS.	10 PER CENT.	5 PER CENT.	8 PER CENT.
960.00	480.00	560.00	1	800.00	400.00	640.00
1920.00	960.00	1120.00	2	1600.00	800.00	1280.00
2880.00	1440.00	1680.00	3	2400.00	1200.00	1920.00
3840.00	1920.00	2240.00	4	3200.00	1600.00	2560.00
4800.00	2400.00	2800.00	5	4000.00	2000.00	3200.00
			MONTHS.			
80.00	40.00	46.67	1	66.67	33.33	53.33
160.00	80.00	93.33	2	133.33	66.67	106.67
240.00	120.00	140.00	3	200.00	100.00	160.00
320.00	160.00	186.67	4	266.67	133.33	213.33
400.00	200.00	233.33	5	333.33	166.67	266.67
480.00	240.00	280.00	**6**	400.00	200.00	320.00
560.00	280.00	326.67	7	466.67	233.33	373.33
640.00	320.00	373.33	8	533.33	266.67	426.67
720.00	360.00	420.00	9	600.00	300.00	480.00
800.00	400 00	466.67	10	666.67	333.33	533.33
880.00	440.00	513.33	11	733.33	366.67	586.67
			DAYS.			
2.67	1.33	1.56	1	2.22	1.11	1.78
5.33	2.67	3.11	2	4.44	2.22	3.56
8.00	4.00	4.67	3	6.67	3.33	5.33
10.67	5.33	6.22	4	8.89	4.44	7.11
13.33	6.67	7.78	**5**	11.11	5.56	8.89
16.00	8.00	9.33	6	13.33	6.67	10.67
18.67	9.33	10.89	7	15.56	7.78	12.44
21.33	10.67	12.44	8	17.78	8.89	14.22
24.00	12.00	14.00	9	20.00	10.00	16.00
26.67	13.33	15.56	**10**	22.22	11.11	17.78
29.33	14.67	17.11	11	24.44	12.22	19.56
32.00	16.00	18.67	12	26.67	13.33	21.33
34.67	17.33	20.22	13	28.89	14.44	23.11
37.33	18.67	21.78	14	31.11	15.56	24.89
40.00	20.00	23.33	**15**	33.33	16.67	26.67
42.67	21.33	24.89	16	35.56	17.78	28.44
45.33	22.67	26 44	17	37.78	18.89	30.22
48.00	24.00	28.00	18	40.00	20.00	32.00
50.67	25.33	29.56	19	42.22	21.11	33.78
53 33	26.67	31.11	**20**	44.44	22.22	35.56
56.00	28.00	32.67	21	46.67	23.33	37.33
58.67	29.33	34.22	22	48.89	24.44	39.11
61.33	30.67	35.78	23	51.11	25.56	40.89
64.00	32.00	37.33	24	53.33	26.67	42.67
66.67	33.33	38.89	**25**	55.56	27.78	44.44
69.33	34.67	40.44	26	57.78	28.89	46.22
72.00	36.00	42.00	27	60.00	30.00	48.00
74.67	37.33	43.56	28	62.22	31.11	49.78
77.33	38.67	45.11	29	64.44	32.22	51.56
80.00	40.00	46.67	**30**	66.67	33.33	53.33
88.00	44.00	51.33	33	73.33	36.67	58.67
168.00	84.00	98.00	63	140.00	70.00	112.00
248 00	124.00	144.67	93	206.67	103.33	165.33

9,000 Dollars.

12 PER CENT.	6 PER CENT.	7 PER CENT.	YEARS.	10 PER CENT.	5 PER CENT.	8 PER CENT.
1080.00	540.00	630.00	1	900.00	450.00	720.00
2160.00	1080.00	1260.00	2	1800.00	900.00	1440.00
3240.00	1620.00	1890.00	3	2700.00	1350.00	2160.00
4320.00	2160.00	2520.00	4	3600.00	1800.00	2880.00
5400.00	2700.00	3150.00	5	4500.00	2250.00	3600.00
			MONTHS.			
90.00	45.00	52.50	1	75.00	37.50	60.00
180.00	90.00	105.00	2	150.00	75.00	120.00
270.00	135.00	157.50	3	225.00	112.50	180.00
360.00	180.00	210.00	4	300.00	150.00	240.00
450.00	225.00	262.50	5	375.00	187.50	300.00
540.00	270.00	315.00	**6**	450.00	225.00	360.00
630.00	315.00	367.50	7	525.00	262.50	420.00
720.00	360.00	420.00	8	600.00	300.00	480.00
810.00	405.00	472.50	9	675.00	337.50	540.00
900.00	450.00	525.00	10	750.00	375.00	600.00
990.00	495.00	577.50	11	825.00	412.50	660.00
			DAYS.			
3.00	1.50	1.75	1	2.50	1.25	2.00
6.00	3.00	3.50	2	5.00	2.50	4.00
9.00	4.50	5.25	3	7.50	3.75	6.00
12.00	6.00	7.00	4	10.00	5.00	8.00
15.00	7.50	8.75	**5**	12.50	6.25	10.00
18.00	9.00	10.50	6	15.00	7.50	12.00
21.00	10.50	12.25	7	17.50	8.75	14.00
24.00	12.00	14.00	8	20.00	10.00	16.00
27.00	13.50	15.75	9	22.50	11.25	18.00
30.00	15.00	17.50	**10**	25.00	12.50	20.00
33.00	16.50	19.25	11	27.50	13.75	22.00
36.00	18.00	21.00	12	30.00	15.00	24.00
39.00	19.50	22.75	13	32.50	16.25	26.00
42.00	21.00	24.50	14	35.00	17.50	28.00
45.00	22.50	26.25	**15**	37.50	18.75	30.00
48.00	24.00	28.00	16	40.00	20.00	32.00
51.00	25.50	29.75	17	42.50	21.25	34.00
54.00	27.00	31.50	18	45.00	22.50	36.00
57.00	28.50	33.25	19	47.50	23.75	38.00
60.00	30.00	35.00	**20**	50.00	25.00	40.00
63.00	31.50	36.75	21	52.50	26.25	42.00
66.00	33.00	38.50	22	55.00	27.50	44.00
69.00	34.50	40.25	23	57.50	28.75	46.00
72.00	36.00	42.00	24	60.00	30.00	48.00
75.00	37.50	43.75	**25**	62.50	31.25	50.00
78.00	39.00	45.50	26	65.00	32.50	52.00
81.00	40.50	47.25	27	67.50	33.75	54.00
84.00	42.00	49.00	28	70.00	35.00	56.00
87.00	43.50	50.75	29	72.50	36.25	58.00
90.00	45.00	52.50	**30**	75.00	37.50	60.00
99.00	49.50	57 75	33	82.50	41.25	66.00
189.00	94.50	110.25	63	157.50	78.75	126.00
279.00	139.50	162.75	93	232.50	116.25	186.00

10,000 Dollars.

12 PER CENT.	6 PER CENT.	7 PER CEMT.	YEARS.	10 PER CENT.	5 PER CENT.	8 PER CENT
1200.00	600.00	700.00	1	1000.00	500.00	800.00
2400.00	1200.00	1400.00	2	2000.00	1000.00	1600.00
3600.00	1800.00	2100.00	3	3000.00	1500.00	2400.00
4800.00	2400.00	2800.00	4	4000.00	2000.00	3200.00
6000.00	3000.00	3500.00	5	5000.00	2500.00	4000.00
			MONTHS.			
100.00	50.00	58.33	1	83.33	41.67	66.67
200.00	100.00	116.67	2	166.67	83.33	133.33
300.00	150.00	175.00	3	250.00	125.00	200.00
400.00	200.00	233.33	4	333.33	166.67	266.67
500.00	250.00	291.67	5	416.67	208.33	333.33
600.00	300.00	350.00	**6**	500.00	250.00	400.00
700.00	350.00	408.33	7	583.33	291.67	466.67
800.00	400.00	466.67	8	666.67	333.33	533.33
900.00	450.00	525.00	9	750.00	375.00	600.00
1000.00	500.00	583.33	10	833.33	416.67	666.67
1100.00	550.00	641.67	11	916.67	458.33	733.33
			DAYS.			
3.33	1.67	1.94	1	2.76	1.38	2.22
6.67	3.33	3.88	2	5.55	2.77	4.44
10.00	5.00	5.83	3	8.33	4.16	6.67
13.33	6.67	7.78	4	11.11	5.55	8.89
16.67	8.33	9.72	**5**	13.88	6.94	11.11
20.00	10.00	11.66	6	16.66	8.33	13.33
23.33	11.67	13.61	7	19.44	9.72	15.56
26.67	13.33	15.56	8	22.22	11.11	17.78
30.00	15.00	17.50	9	25.00	12.50	20.00
33.33	16.67	19.44	**10**	27.77	13.88	22.22
36.67	18.33	21.38	11	30.55	15.27	24.44
40.00	20.00	23.33	12	33.33	16.66	26.67
43.33	21.67	25.27	13	36.11	18.05	28.89
46.67	23.33	27.22	14	38.88	19.44	31.11
50.00	25.00	29.16	**15**	41.66	20.83	33.33
53.33	26.67	31.11	16	44.44	22.22	35.56
56.67	28.33	33.06	17	47.22	23.61	37.78
60.00	30.00	35.00	18	50.00	25.00	40.00
63.33	31.66	36.94	19	52.77	26.38	42.22
66.67	33.33	38.88	**20**	55.55	27.77	44.44
70.00	35.00	40.83	21	58.33	29.16	46.67
73.33	36.67	42.77	22	61.11	30.55	48.89
76.67	38.33	44.72	23	63.88	31.94	51.11
80.00	40.00	46.66	24	66.66	33.33	53.33
83.33	41.67	48.61	**25**	69.44	34.72	55.56
86.67	43.33	50.56	26	72.22	36.11	57.78
90.00	45.00	52.50	27	75.00	37.50	60.00
93.33	46.67	54.44	28	77.77	38.88	62.22
96.67	48.33	56.38	29	80.55	40.27	64.44
100.00	50.00	58.33	**30**	83.33	41.66	66.67
110.00	55.00	64.16	63	91.67	45.82	73.34
210.00	105.00	122.50	63	175.00	87.50	140.01
310.00	155.00	180.83	93	258.33	129.16	206.68

TABLE FOR MARKING GOODS.

TABLE IV. (See Introduction.)

	5 Per Cent.	7 Per Cent.	10 Per Cent.	12 1-2 Per Cent.	15 Per Cent.	20 Per Cent.	25 Per Cent.	30 Per Cent.
1	1.05	1.07	1.10	1.125	1.15	1.20	1.25	1.30
2	2.10	2.14	2.20	2.25	2.30	2.40	2.50	2.60
3	3.15	3.21	3.30	3.375	3.45	3.60	3.75	3.90
4	4.20	4.28	4.40	4.50	4.60	4.80	5.00	5.20
5	5.25	5.35	5.50	5.625	5.75	6.00	6.25	6.50
6	6.30	6.42	6.60	6.75	6.90	7.20	7.50	7.80
7	7.35	7.49	7.70	7.875	8.05	8.40	8.75	9.10
8	8.40	8.56	8.80	9.00	9.20	9.60	10.00	10.40
9	9.45	9.63	9.90	10.125	10.35	10.80	11.25	11.70
10	10.50	10.70	11.00	11.25	11.50	12.00	12.50	13.00
11	11.55	11.77	12.10	12.375	12.65	13.20	13.75	14.30
12	12.60	12.84	13.20	13.50	13.80	14.40	15.00	15.60
13	13.65	13.91	14.30	14.625	14.95	15.60	16.25	16.90
14	14.70	14.98	15.40	15.75	16.10	16.80	17.50	18.20
15	15.75	16.05	16.50	16.875	17.25	18.00	18.75	19.50
16	16.80	17.12	17.60	18.00	18.40	19.20	20.00	20.80
17	17.85	18.19	18.70	19.125	19.55	20.40	21.25	22.10
18	18.90	19.26	19.80	20.25	20.70	21.60	22.50	23.40
19	19.95	20.33	20.90	21.375	21.85	22.80	23.75	24.70
20	21.00	21.40	22.00	22.50	23.00	24.00	25.00	26.00
21	22.05	22.47	23.10	23.625	24.15	25.20	26.25	27.30
22	23.10	23.54	24.20	24.75	25.30	26.40	27.50	28.60
23	24.15	24.61	25.30	25.875	26.45	27.60	28.75	29.90
24	25.20	25.68	26.40	27.00	27.60	28.80	30.00	31.20
25	26.25	26.75	27.50	28.125	28.75	30.00	31.25	32.50
26	27.30	27.82	28.60	29.25	29.90	31.20	32.50	33.80
27	28.35	28.89	29.70	30.375	31.05	32.40	33.75	35.10
28	29.40	29.96	30.80	31.50	32.20	33.60	35.00	36.40
29	30.45	31.03	31.90	32.625	33.35	34.80	36.25	37.70
30	31.50	32.10	33.00	33.75	34.50	36.00	37.50	39.00
31	32.55	33.17	34.10	34.875	35.65	37.20	38.75	40.30
32	33.60	34.24	35.20	36.00	36.80	38.40	40.00	41.60
33	34.65	35.31	36.30	37.125	37.95	39.60	41.25	42.90
34	35.70	36.38	37.40	38.25	39.10	40.80	42.50	44.20
35	36.75	37.45	38.50	39.375	40.25	42.00	43.75	45.50
36	37.80	38.52	39.60	40.50	41.40	43.20	45.00	46.80
37	38.85	39.59	40.70	41.625	42.55	44.40	46.25	48.10
38	39.90	40.66	41.80	42.75	43.70	45.60	47.50	49.40
39	40.95	41.73	42.90	43.875	44.85	46.80	48.75	50.70
40	42.00	42.80	44.00	45.00	46.00	48.00	50.00	52.00
41	43.05	43.87	45.10	46.125	47.15	49.20	51.25	53.30
42	44.10	44.94	46.20	47.25	48.30	50.40	52.50	54.60
43	45.15	46.01	47.30	48.375	49.45	51.60	53.75	55.90
44	46.20	47.08	48.40	49.50	50.60	52.80	55.00	57.20
45	47.25	48.15	49.50	50.625	51.75	54.00	56.25	58.50
46	48.30	49.22	50.60	51.75	52.90	55.20	57.50	59.80
47	49.35	50.29	51.70	52.875	54.05	56.40	58.75	61.10
48	50.40	51.36	52.80	54.00	55.20	57.60	60.00	62.40
49	51.45	52.43	53.90	55.125	56.35	58.80	61.25	63.70
50	52.50	53.50	55.00	56.25	57.50	60.00	62.50	65.00

TABLE FOR MARKING GOODS.

	33 1-3 Per Cent.	40 Per Cent.	50 Per Cent.	66 2-3 Per Cent.	75 Per Cent.	100 Per Cent.	150 Per Cent.	200 Per Cent.
1	1.33	1.40	1.50	1.67	1.75	2.00	2.50	3.00
2	2.67	2.80	3.00	3.33	3.50	4.00	5.00	6.00
3	4.00	4.20	4.50	5.00	5.25	6.00	7.50	9.00
4	5.33	5.60	6.00	6.67	7.00	8.00	10.00	12.00
5	6.67	7.00	7.50	8.33	8.75	10.00	12.50	15.00
6	8.00	8.40	9.00	10.00	10.50	12.00	15.00	18.00
7	9.33	9.80	10.50	11.67	12.25	14.00	17.50	21.00
8	10.67	11.20	12.00	13.33	14.00	16.00	20.00	24.00
9	12.00	12.60	13.50	15.00	15.75	18.00	22.50	27.00
10	13.33	14.00	15.00	16.67	17.50	20.00	25.00	30.00
11	14.67	15.40	16.50	18.33	19.25	22.00	27.50	33.00
12	16.00	16.80	18.00	20.00	21.00	24.00	30.00	36.00
13	17.33	18.20	19.50	21.67	22.75	26.00	32.50	39.00
14	18.67	19.60	21.00	23.33	24.50	28.00	35.00	42.00
15	20.00	21.00	22.50	25.00	26.25	30.00	37.50	45.00
16	21.33	22.40	24.00	26.67	28.00	32.00	40.00	48.00
17	22.67	23.80	25.50	28.33	29.75	34.00	42.50	51.00
18	24.00	25.20	27.00	30.00	31.50	36.00	45.00	54.00
19	25.33	26.60	28.50	31.67	33.25	38.00	47.50	57.00
20	26.67	28.00	30.00	33.33	35.00	40.00	50.00	60.00
21	28.00	29.40	31.50	35.00	36.75	42.00	52.50	63.00
22	29.33	30.80	33.00	36.67	38.50	44.00	55.00	66.00
23	30.67	32.20	34.50	38.33	40.25	46.00	57.50	69.00
24	32.00	33.60	36.00	40.00	42.00	48.00	60.00	72.00
25	33.33	35.00	37.50	41.67	43.75	50.00	62.50	75.00
26	34.67	36.40	39.00	43.33	45.50	52.00	65.00	78.00
27	36.00	37.80	40.50	45.00	47.25	54.00	67.50	81.00
28	37.33	39.20	42.00	46.67	49.00	56.00	70.00	84.00
29	38.67	40.60	43.50	48.33	50.75	58.00	72.50	87.00
30	40.00	42.00	45.00	50.00	52.50	60.00	75.00	90.00
31	41.33	43.40	46.50	51.67	54.25	62.00	77.50	93.00
32	42.67	44.80	48.00	53.33	56.00	64.00	80.00	96.00
33	44.00	46.20	49.50	55.00	57.75	66.00	82.50	99.00
34	45.33	47.60	51.00	56.67	59.50	68.00	85.00	102.00
35	46.67	49.00	52.50	58.33	61.25	70.00	87.50	105.00
36	48.00	50.40	54.00	60.00	63.00	72.00	90.00	108.00
37	49.33	51.80	55.50	61.67	64.75	74.00	92.50	111.00
38	50.67	53.20	57.00	63.33	66.50	76.00	95.00	114.00
39	52.00	54.60	58.50	65.00	68.25	78.00	97.50	117.00
40	53.33	56.00	60.00	66.67	70.00	80.00	100.00	120.00
41	54.67	57.40	61.50	68.33	71.75	82.00	102.50	123.00
42	56.00	58.80	63.00	70.00	73.50	84.00	105.00	126.00
43	57.33	60.20	64.50	71.67	75.25	86.00	107.50	129.00
44	58.67	61.60	66.00	73.33	77.00	88.00	110.00	132.00
45	60.00	63.00	67.50	75.00	78.75	90.00	112.50	135.00
46	61.33	64.40	69.00	76.67	80.50	92.00	115.00	138.00
47	62.67	65.80	70.50	78.33	82.25	94.00	117.50	141.00
48	64.00	67.20	72.00	80.00	84.00	96.00	120.00	144.00
49	65.33	68.60	73.50	81.67	85.75	98.00	122.50	147.00
50	66.67	70.00	75.00	83.33	87.50	100.00	125.00	150.00

TABLE FOR MARKING GOODS.

	5 Per Cent.	7 Per Cent.	10 Per Cent.	12 1-2 Per Cent.	15 Per Cent.	20 Per Cent.	25 Per Cent.	30 Per Cent.
51	53.55	54.57	56.10	57.375	58.65	61.20	63.75	66.30
52	54.60	55.64	57.20	58.50	59.80	62.40	65.00	67.60
53	55.65	56.71	58.30	59.625	60.95	63.60	66.25	68.90
54	56.70	57.78	59.40	60.75	62.10	64.80	67.50	70.20
55	57.75	58.85	60.50	61.875	63.25	66.00	68.75	71.50
56	58.80	59.92	61.60	63.00	64.40	67.20	70.00	72.80
57	59.85	60.99	62.70	64.125	65.55	68.40	71.25	74.10
58	60.90	62.06	63.80	65.25	66.70	69.60	72.50	75.40
59	61.95	63.13	64.90	66.375	67.85	70.80	73.75	76.70
60	63.00	64.20	66.00	67.50	69.00	72.00	75.00	78.00
61	64.05	65.27	67.10	68.625	70.15	73.20	76.25	79.30
62	65.10	66.34	68.20	69.75	71.30	74.40	77.50	80.60
63	66.15	67.41	69.30	70.875	72.45	75.60	78.75	81.90
64	67.20	68.48	70.40	72.00	73.60	76.80	80.00	83.20
65	68.25	69.55	71.50	73.125	74.75	78.00	81.25	84.50
66	69.30	70.62	72.60	74.25	75.90	79.20	82.50	85.80
67	70.35	71.69	73.70	75.375	77.05	80.40	83.75	87.10
68	71.40	72.76	74.80	76.50	78.20	81.60	85.00	88.40
69	72.45	73.83	75.90	77.625	79.35	82.80	86.25	89.70
70	73.50	74.90	77.00	78.75	80.50	84.00	87.50	91.00
71	74.55	75.97	78.10	79.875	81.65	85.20	88.75	92.30
72	75.60	77.04	79.20	81.00	82.80	86.40	90.00	93.60
73	76.65	78.11	80.30	82.125	83.95	87.60	91.25	94.90
74	77.70	79.18	81.40	83.25	85.10	88.80	92.50	96.20
75	78.75	80.25	82.50	84.375	86.25	90.00	93.75	97.50
76	79.80	81.32	83.60	85.50	87.40	91.20	95.00	98.80
77	80.85	82.39	84.70	86.625	88.55	92.40	96.25	100.10
78	81.90	83.46	85.80	87.75	89.70	93.60	97.50	101.40
79	82.95	84.53	86.90	88.875	90.85	94.80	98.75	102.70
80	84.00	85.60	88.00	90.00	92.00	96.00	100.00	104.00
81	85.05	86.67	89.10	91.125	93.15	97.20	101.25	105.30
82	86.10	87.74	90.20	92.25	94.30	98.40	102.50	106.60
83	87.15	88.81	91.30	93.375	95.45	99.60	103.75	107.90
84	88.20	89.88	92.40	94.50	96.60	100.80	105.00	109.20
85	89.25	90.95	93.50	95.625	97.75	102.00	106.25	110.50
86	90.30	92.02	94.60	96.75	98.90	103.20	107.50	111.80
87	91.35	93.09	95.70	97.875	100.05	104.40	108.75	113.10
88	92.40	94.16	96.80	99.00	101.20	105.60	110.00	114.40
89	93.45	95.23	97.90	100.125	102.35	106.80	111.25	115.70
90	94.50	96.30	99.00	101.25	103.50	108.00	112.50	117.00
91	95.55	97.37	100.10	102.375	104.65	109.20	113.75	118.30
92	96.60	98.44	101.20	103.50	105.80	110.40	115.00	119.60
93	97.65	99.51	102.30	104.625	106.95	111.60	116.25	120.90
94	98.70	100.58	103.40	105.75	108.10	112.80	117.50	122.20
95	99.75	101.65	104.50	106.875	109.25	114.00	118.75	123.50
96	100.80	102.72	105.60	108.00	110.40	115.20	120.00	124.80
97	101.85	103.79	106.70	109.125	111.55	116.40	121.25	126.10
98	102.90	104.86	107.80	110.25	112.70	117.60	122.50	127.40
99	103.95	105.93	108.90	111.375	113.85	118.80	123.75	128.70
100	105.00	107.00	110.00	112.50	115.00	120.00	125.00	130.00

TABLE FOR MARKING GOODS.

	33 1-3 Per Cent.	40 Per Cent.	50 Per Cent.	66 2-3 Per Cent.	75 Per Cent.	100 Per Cent.	150 Per Cent.	200 Per Cent.
51	68.00	71.40	76.50	85.00	89.25	102.00	127.50	153.00
52	69.33	72.80	78.00	86.67	91.00	104.00	130.00	156.00
53	70.67	74.20	79.50	88.33	92.75	106.00	132.50	159.00
54	72.00	75.60	81.00	90.00	94.50	108.00	135.00	162.00
55	73.33	77.00	82.50	91.67	96.25	110.00	137.50	165.00
56	74.67	78.40	84.00	93.33	98.00	112.00	140.00	168.00
57	76.00	79.80	85.50	95.00	99.75	114.00	142.50	171.00
58	77.33	81.20	87.00	96.67	101.50	116.00	145.00	174.00
59	78.67	82.60	88.50	98.33	103.25	118.00	147.50	177.00
60	80.00	84.00	90.00	100.00	105.00	120.00	150.00	180.00
61	81.33	85.40	91.50	101.67	106.75	122.00	152.50	183.00
62	82.67	86.80	93.00	103.33	108.50	124.00	155.00	186.00
63	84.00	88.20	94.50	105.00	110.25	126.00	157.50	189.00
64	85.33	89.60	96.00	106.67	112.00	128.00	160.00	192.00
65	86.67	91.00	97.50	108.33	113.75	130.00	162.50	195.00
66	88.00	92.40	99.00	110.00	115.50	132.00	165.00	198.00
67	89.33	93.80	100.50	111.67	117.25	134.00	167.50	201.00
68	90.67	95.20	102.00	113.33	119.00	136.00	170.00	204.00
69	92.00	96.60	103.50	115.00	120.75	138.00	172.50	207.00
70	93.33	98.00	105.00	116.67	122.50	140.00	175.00	210.00
71	94.67	99.40	106.50	118.33	124.25	142.00	177.50	213.00
72	96.00	100.80	108.00	120.00	126.00	144.00	180.00	216.00
73	97.33	102.20	109.50	121.67	127.75	146.00	182.50	219.00
74	98.67	103.60	111.00	123.33	129.50	148.00	185.00	222.00
75	100.00	105.00	112.50	125.00	131.25	150.00	187.50	225.00
76	101.33	106.40	114.00	126.67	133,00	152.00	190.00	228.00
77	102.67	107.80	115.50	128.33	134.75	154.00	192.50	231.00
78	104.00	109.20	117.00	130.00	136.50	156.00	195.00	234.00
79	105.33	110.60	118.50	131.67	138.25	158.00	197.50	237.00
80	106.67	112.00	120.00	133.33	140.00	160.00	200.00	240.00
81	108.00	113.40	121.50	135.00	141.75	162.00	202.50	243.00
82	109.33	114.80	123.00	136.67	143.50	164.00	205.00	246.00
83	110.67	116.20	124.50	138.33	145.25	166.00	207.50	249.00
84	112.00	117.60	126.00	140.00	147.00	168.00	210.00	252.00
85	113.33	119.00	127.50	141.67	148.75	170.00	212.50	255.00
86	114.67	120.40	129.00	143.33	150.50	172.00	215.00	258.00
87	116.00	121.80	130.50	145.00	152.25	174.00	217.50	261.00
88	117.33	123.20	132.00	146.67	154.00	176.00	220.00	264.00
89	118.67	124.60	133.50	148.33	155.75	178.00	222.50	267.00
90	120.00	126.00	135.00	150.00	157.50	180.00	225.00	270.00
91	121.33	127.40	136.50	151.67	159.25	182.00	227.50	273.00
92	122.67	128.80	138.00	153.33	161.00	184.00	230.00	276.00
93	124.00	130.20	139.50	155.00	162.75	186.00	232.50	279.00
94	125.33	131.60	141.00	156.67	164.50	188.00	235.00	282.00
95	126.67	133.00	142.50	158.33	166.25	190.00	237.50	285.00
96	128.00	134.40	144.00	160.00	168.00	192.00	240.00	288.00
97	129.33	135.80	145.50	161.67	169.75	194.00	242.50	291.00
98	130.67	137.20	147.00	163.33	171.50	196.00	245.00	294.00
99	132.00	138.60	148.50	165.00	173.25	198.00	247.50	297.00
100	133.33	140.00	150.00	166.67	175.00	200.00	250.00	300.00

TIME TABLE NO. V.

(SEE INTRODUCTION.)

JAN.	FEB.	MAR.	APRIL	MAY	JUNE	JULY	AUG.	SEPT.	OCT.	NOV.	DEC.
1	1	1	1	1	1	1	1	1	1	1	1
1	32	60	91	121	152	182	213	244	274	305	335
2	2	2	2	2	2	2	2	2	2	2	2
2	33	61	92	122	153	183	214	245	275	306	336
3	3	3	3	3	3	3	3	3	3	3	3
3	34	62	93	123	154	184	215	246	276	307	337
4	4	4	4	4	4	4	4	4	4	4	4
4	35	63	94	124	155	185	216	247	277	308	338
5	5	5	5	5	5	5	5	5	5	5	5
5	36	64	95	125	156	186	217	248	278	309	339
6	6	6	6	6	6	6	6	6	6	6	6
6	37	65	96	126	157	187	218	249	279	310	340
7	7	7	7	7	7	7	7	7	7	7	7
7	38	66	97	127	158	188	219	250	280	311	341
8	8	8	8	8	8	8	8	8	8	8	8
8	39	67	98	128	159	189	220	251	281	212	342
9	9	9	9	9	9	9	9	9	9	9	9
9	40	68	99	129	160	190	221	252	282	313	343
10	10	10	10	10	10	10	10	10	10	10	10
10	41	69	100	130	161	191	222	253	283	314	344
11	11	11	11	11	11	11	11	11	11	11	11
11	42	70	101	131	162	192	223	254	284	315	345
12	12	12	12	12	12	12	12	12	12	12	12
12	43	71	102	132	163	193	224	255	285	316	346
13	13	13	13	13	13	13	13	13	13	13	13
13	44	72	103	133	164	194	225	256	286	317	347
14	14	14	14	14	14	14	14	14	14	14	14
14	45	73	104	134	165	195	226	257	287	318	348
15	15	15	15	15	15	15	15	15	15	15	15
15	46	74	105	135	166	196	227	258	288	319	349
16	16	16	16	16	16	16	16	16	16	16	16
16	47	75	106	136	167	197	228	259	289	320	350
17	17	17	17	17	17	17	17	17	17	17	17
17	48	76	107	137	168	198	229	260	290	321	351
18	18	18	18	18	18	18	18	18	18	18	18
18	49	77	108	138	169	199	230	261	291	322	352
19	19	19	19	19	19	19	19	19	19	19	19
19	50	78	109	139	170	200	231	262	292	323	353
20	20	20	20	20	20	20	20	20	20	20	20
20	51	79	110	140	171	201	232	263	293	324	354
21	21	21	21	21	21	21	21	21	21	21	21
21	52	80	111	141	172	202	233	264	294	325	355
22	22	22	22	22	22	22	22	22	22	22	22
22	53	81	112	142	173	203	234	265	295	326	356
23	23	23	23	23	23	23	23	23	23	23	23
23	54	82	113	143	174	204	235	266	296	327	357
24	24	24	24	24	24	24	24	24	24	24	24
24	55	83	114	144	175	205	236	267	297	328	358
25	25	25	25	25	25	25	25	25	25	25	25
25	56	84	115	145	176	206	237	268	298	329	359
26	26	26	26	26	26	26	26	26	26	26	26
26	57	85	116	146	177	207	238	269	299	330	360
27	27	27	27	27	27	27	27	27	27	27	27
27	58	86	117	147	178	208	239	270	300	331	361
28	28	28	28	28	28	28	28	28	28	28	28
28	59	87	118	148	179	209	240	271	301	332	362
29		29	29	29	29	29	29	29	29	29	29
29		88	119	149	180	210	241	272	302	333	363
30		30	30	30	30	30	30	30	30	30	30
30		89	120	150	181	211	242	273	303	334	364
31		31		31		31	31		31		31
31		90		151		212	243		304		365

TIME TABLE NO. V.

(SEE INTRODUCTION.)

JAN.	FEB.	MAR.	APRIL	MAY	JUNE	JULY	AUG.	SEPT.	OCT.	NOV.	DEC.
1	1	1	1	1	1	1	1	1	1	1	1
366	397	425	456	486	517	547	578	609	639	670	700
2	2	2	2	2	2	2	2	2	2	2	2
367	398	426	457	487	518	548	579	610	640	671	701
3	3	3	3	3	3	3	3	3	3	3	3
368	399	427	458	488	519	549	580	611	641	672	702
4	4	4	4	4	4	4	4	4	4	4	4
369	400	428	459	489	520	550	581	612	642	673	703
5	5	5	5	5	5	5	5	5	5	5	5
370	401	429	460	490	521	551	282	613	643	674	704
6	6	6	6	6	6	6	6	6	6	6	6
371	402	430	461	491	522	552	283	614	644	675	705
7	7	7	7	7	7	7	7	7	7	7	7
372	403	431	462	492	523	553	584	615	645	676	706
8	8	8	8	8	8	8	8	8	8	8	8
373	404	432	463	493	524	554	585	616	646	677	707
9	9	9	9	9	9	9	9	9	9	9	9
374	405	433	464	494	525	555	586	617	647	678	708
10	10	10	10	10	10	10	10	10	10	10	10
375	406	434	465	495	526	556	587	618	648	679	709
11	11	11	11	11	11	11	11	11	11	11	11
376	407	435	466	596	527	557	588	619	649	680	710
12	12	12	12	12	12	12	12	12	12	12	12
377	408	436	467	497	528	558	589	620	650	681	711
13	13	13	13	13	13	13	13	13	13	13	13
378	409	437	468	498	529	559	590	621	651	682	712
14	14	14	14	14	14	14	14	14	14	14	14
379	410	438	469	499	530	560	591	622	652	683	713
15	15	15	15	15	15	15	15	15	15	15	15
380	411	439	470	500	531	561	592	623	653	684	714
16	16	16	16	16	16	16	16	16	16	16	16
381	412	440	471	501	532	562	593	624	654	685	715
17	17	17	17	17	17	17	17	17	17	17	17
382	413	441	472	502	533	563	594	625	655	686	716
18	18	18	18	18	18	18	18	18	18	18	18
383	414	442	473	503	534	564	595	626	656	687	717
19	19	19	19	19	19	19	19	19	19	19	19
384	415	443	474	504	535	565	596	627	657	688	718
20	20	20	20	20	20	20	20	20	20	20	20
385	416	444	475	505	536	566	597	628	658	689	719
21	21	21	21	21	21	21	21	21	21	21	21
386	417	445	476	506	537	567	598	629	659	690	720
22	22	22	22	22	22	22	22	22	22	22	22
387	418	446	477	507	538	568	599	630	660	691	721
23	23	23	23	23	23	23	23	23	23	23	23
388	419	447	478	508	839	569	600	631	661	692	722
24	24	24	24	24	24	24	24	24	24	24	24
389	420	448	479	509	540	570	601	632	662	693	723
25	25	25	25	25	25	25	25	25	25	25	25
390	421	449	480	510	541	571	602	633	663	694	724
26	26	26	26	26	26	26	26	26	26	26	26
391	422	450	481	511	542	572	603	634	564	695	725
27	27	27	27	27	27	27	27	27	27	27	27
392	423	451	482	512	543	573	604	635	665	696	726
28	28	28	28	28	28	28	28	28	28	28	28
393	424	452	483	513	544	574	605	636	666	697	727
29		29	29	29	29	29	29	29	29	29	29
394		453	484	514	545	275	606	637	667	698	728
30		30	30	30	30	30	30	30	30	30	30
395		454	485	515	546	276	607	638	668	699	729
31		31		31		31	31		31		31
396		455		516		277	608		669		730

EQUATION OF PAYMENTS.

TABLE IV.

RULE.—Multiply each amount by the time to elapse before it becomes due; divide the sum of these products by the sum of the amounts.

ILLUSTRATION I.

A. buys goods of B. as follows, on 60 days' time: July 10th, $70; July 25th, $105; Aug. 8th, $90; Aug. 15th, $40. Sept. 1st, he wishes to give a note covering the entire indebtedness; for what time shall it be given?

AMOUNTS.	DAYS.	PRODUCTS
$ 70	10	700
105	25	2625
90	38	3420
40	45	1800
$305		8545 ÷ 305 = 24.7+

Seven-tenths being greater than one-half should be reckoned as one day, and the note given for 25 days.

ILLUSTRATION II.

C. buys goods of D. as follows, on 90 days' credit: April 1st, $100; April 20th, $250; May 10th, $95; May 25th, $225; June 10th, $55; June 13th, $175. For what length of time should a note covering the entire indebtedness be given July 1st?

AMOUNTS.	DAYS.	PRODUCTS.
$100	0	0
250	20	5000
95	40	3800
225	55	12375
55	70	3850
175	73	12775
$900		37800 ÷ 900 = 42

www.ingramcontent.com/pod-product-compliance
Lightning Source LLC
LaVergne TN
LVHW021417110826
845150LV00007B/1973

* 9 7 8 1 4 2 5 5 0 9 7 2 9 *